INTRODUCTION

In 2019, I made one of the boldest decisions of my life—I quit my job as a 2nd Officer in the Merchant Navy to follow my dream of becoming an entrepreneur. It wasn't an easy choice. The Merchant Navy gave me stability and adventure, but something didn't feel right. I craved freedom—the freedom to build my own dreams instead of working for someone else's, to make my own rules, and to take control of my life.

Entrepreneurship wasn't just a career shift for me; it was a necessity. I needed to create something meaningful on my own terms. Since then, I've been on an exhilarating journey of building businesses and helping others grow theirs. Over the years, I've experienced the highs and lows of being an entrepreneur— learning lessons, facing challenges, and celebrating successes along the way.

This book is my way of sharing everything I've learned, so you don't have to start blind like I did. Whether you're someone who's dreaming of starting a business or are already on the path and looking for guidance, this book will serve as a roadmap to help you navigate the journey.

Through these pages, I'll show you how to go from an idea to building a thriving business. From finding the right idea and choosing the best legal structure to acquiring customers, raising funds, and planning your exit strategy—this book is packed with practical advice, actionable tips, and real-life insights.

The journey of entrepreneurship isn't easy, but it's incredibly rewarding. If you've ever felt stuck in a system that doesn't inspire you or dreamed of having the freedom to create something impactful, this book is for you.

Remember, every great business begins with a single decision—the decision to start. Let's take that step together and build something extraordinary.

Welcome to the journey.

Animesh

Published by:
GroWithAnimesh
India

First Edition
February, 2025

Cover Design by Animesh Kumar

For inquiries or permissions, contact: growithanimesh@gmail.com

Do not wait; the time will never be 'just right.' Start where you stand, and work with whatever tools you may have."

– Napoleon Hill

Dedication

To every dreamer who dares to believe in their vision and takes the leap into entrepreneurship.

To the hustlers who work tirelessly to turn ideas into reality, embracing failures as lessons and successes as milestones.

And to my family, friends, and mentors, whose unwavering support and guidance have made this journey possible.

This book is for you—because every great startup starts with a dream and relentless passion.

Table of Contents

INTRODUCTION

Why Startups Matter

Startups are more than just businesses—they are the lifeblood of innovation, progress, and change. They challenge the status quo, solve real problems, and shape the future. Think about it: the apps you use, the gadgets you rely on, and even the services that simplify your life—all began as someone's idea.

But here's the thing—building a startup isn't just for tech wizards or billionaires. It's for anyone with a vision, a strong work ethic, and the willingness to learn. Your startup has the potential to not only change your life but also positively impact the lives of others.

The beauty of entrepreneurship is that it's open to everyone, regardless of your background or resources. When I left my job in the Merchant Navy, I had no business degree or experience in startups. What I did have was a passion for freedom and a hunger to create something meaningful.

And that's what this book is about: showing you that you, too, can take your idea, build it step by step, and turn it into a thriving business.

How This Book Will Help You

This isn't just a collection of theories or abstract advice. It's a practical guide filled with actionable steps, insights from real-world experience, and lessons from successful entrepreneurs. Whether you're at the idea stage, trying to build momentum, or looking to scale your business, you'll find tools and strategies that can be applied immediately.

As we move forward, I'll share lessons I've learned from my own entrepreneurial journey, from leaving a secure job to creating and scaling businesses. You'll also find case studies, relatable examples, and exercises that will help you turn your ideas into a solid, actionable plan.

This isn't just a book—it's a companion on your journey. So, buckle up and get ready to turn your dreams into reality.

The Entrepreneurial Mindset

Starting a business isn't just about having a great idea; it's about having the right mindset to execute it. Success in entrepreneurship isn't guaranteed by luck or timing alone—it's about how you think, adapt, and persist when things get tough.

When I quit my Merchant Navy job in 2019, I was stepping into the unknown. I didn't have a safety net or the answers to every question, but I had the willingness to learn, take calculated risks, and trust myself. That mindset made all the difference.

Here are a few key principles of the entrepreneurial mindset that will shape your journey:

1. **Adaptability**: The startup world is unpredictable. Your ability to pivot, embrace change, and find opportunities in challenges will set you apart.

- ○ *Example*: When I faced setbacks in my early days as an entrepreneur, I learned to view them as lessons rather than failures. Each obstacle pushed me to rethink strategies and move forward stronger.

2. **Resilience**: You will encounter rejections, failures, and tough days. Resilience will keep you moving forward when the odds are stacked against you.

   - ○ *Think about this*: Every big success story you admire—from Steve Jobs to Dhirubhai Ambani—started with countless failures that were overcome with grit.

3. **Curiosity**: The most successful entrepreneurs are lifelong learners. Curiosity keeps you innovating and helps you understand markets, customers, and industries.

   - ○ *Tip*: Read books, listen to podcasts, and network with other entrepreneurs. Learning doesn't stop once you start your business—it accelerates.

4. **Action-Oriented Thinking**: It's easy to overthink and delay starting. But ideas are worthless without execution. Focus on taking small, consistent steps every day.

   - ○ *Ask yourself*: What's one thing I can do today to move closer to my goal?

5. **Customer-Centric Approach**: Great businesses solve real problems for real people. Always keep your customers at the center of your decisions.

   - ○ *Insight*: If you're building something you wouldn't buy or use yourself, rethink your approach.

Overcoming the Fear of Starting

It's natural to feel scared or overwhelmed at the beginning. What if I fail? What if I don't have the skills or resources? These are questions every entrepreneur faces. But here's a secret: the fear never goes away completely—you just learn to move forward despite it.

Start small. Break the big picture into manageable tasks. Focus on progress, not perfection. The key is to take action and learn as you go. You don't have to know everything to begin; you just need the courage to start.

Remember, even the most successful entrepreneurs started with nothing but a dream and determination. If they can do it, so can you.

CHAPTER 1

FINDING THE RIGHT IDEA

Every successful startup begins with an idea. But not every idea is worth pursuing. The difference between a passing thought and a viable business idea lies in how you evaluate, refine, and act on it.

When I started my entrepreneurial journey, I had plenty of ideas. Some sounded exciting, but not all of them were practical or scalable. Through trial and error, I realized that the right idea isn't just about what excites you—it's about what solves a real problem.

Here's a step-by-step guide to help you identify and shape your idea:

1. Identify Problems Around You

The best businesses solve real problems. Look around you—what's frustrating people? What gaps exist in the market?

Three Types of Problems to Solve:

1. **Pain Points**: Problems people face daily (e.g., unreliable transportation → Ola/Uber).

2. **Inefficiencies**: Processes that take too much time, money, or effort (e.g., slow food ordering → Swiggy).

3. **Aspirations**: Meeting desires people didn't know they had (e.g., personalized beauty products → Nykaa).

Action Step: Spend a week observing your daily life and talking to people about their challenges. Write down potential problems you could solve.

2. Play to Your Strengths

Your startup should leverage your skills, interests, and experiences. This gives you a natural edge over competitors.

- *Insight*: My background in the Merchant Navy taught me discipline, attention to detail, and decision-making under pressure—all of which helped me as an entrepreneur.

Action Step: List your skills, experiences, and passions. Match them with the problems you've identified.

3. Validate Your Idea

An idea isn't valuable until it's validated. This means testing whether people are willing to pay for your solution.

- *Tip*: Don't assume people need your product—ask them! Conduct surveys, talk to potential customers, or create a simple prototype to gather feedback.

Example:

- Zomato started as a small website where restaurant menus were uploaded for convenience. The founders tested it in their local area before expanding.

- Dropbox validated its idea with a simple demo video before building the product. This generated early interest and convinced investors.
- Mamaearth began with a small product line to test demand for toxin-free baby care products before scaling.

Action Step: Draft a simple survey or talk to 20 people in your target audience to see if they'd pay for your solution.

4. Assess Market Potential

Even a great idea can fail if the market isn't big enough. Research the size of your target market, trends, and competition.

TAM-SAM-SOM Framework:

1. **TAM (Total Addressable Market)**: The total market size if everyone used your product.

2. **SAM (Serviceable Addressable Market)**: The portion of the market you can realistically target.

3. **SOM (Serviceable Obtainable Market)**: The portion you can actually capture in the short term.

Example:

- TAM for an online education platform in India could be all students across the country.
- SAM might be high-school students in Tier-1 and Tier-2 cities.
- SOM could be 10% of this segment initially.

Action Step: Use tools like Google Trends, industry reports, and customer feedback to analyze the market.

5. Start Small and Iterate

You don't need to build a perfect product on day one. Start with a minimum viable product (MVP)—a basic version of your solution—and improve it based on feedback.

- *Example*: Airbnb started with air mattresses in a single apartment. They tested their idea before growing into the global giant it is today.

Action Step: Focus on creating a simple prototype of your product or service. Launch it to a small group of users and gather feedback.

Key Questions to Ask Yourself:

- Does my idea solve a real problem?

- Who is my target customer?

- Are people willing to pay for this solution?

- Can I build a sustainable and scalable business around this idea?

Real-Life Case Study

Case Study: Airbnb's Early Days

- **Problem**: Expensive hotels during events left many people without affordable accommodation.

- **Solution**: The founders started with an air mattress and a website, "AirBed & Breakfast," to test the idea.

- **Validation**: They received early bookings from event attendees and expanded based on feedback.

- **Lesson**: Start small and solve a specific problem for a niche audience before scaling.

From Idea to Execution

The gap between a great idea and a thriving business lies in execution. It's not enough to dream big—you need to act consistently. Start small, focus on solving problems, and learn from every step of the journey.

Remember, every big company you admire today—whether it's Google, Amazon, or Flipkart—started small. They began with an idea, validated it, and worked tirelessly to bring it to life.

Your journey is no different. The next step is to refine your idea and start building a foundation for your business. Let's move forward together.

CHAPTER 2

BUILDING A SOLID FOUNDATION

Setting a Clear Vision and Mission

Before diving into the technicalities of legal structures, it's crucial to define your startup's purpose. Your vision and mission act as a compass, guiding every decision you make.

- **Vision**: This is your long-term goal—what you aim to achieve in the future.
  Example: Tesla's vision is "to create the most compelling car company of the 21st century by driving the world's transition to electric vehicles."

- **Mission**: This is how you plan to achieve your vision.
  Example: Google's mission is "to organize the world's information and make It universally accessible and useful."

Choosing Your Co-Founders and Team

Starting a business can be overwhelming, which is why many founders team up with co-founders. However, the right team isn't just about skills—it's about shared values, trust, and complementary strengths.

Traits to Look for in Co-Founders

1. ***Complementary Skills***: Ensure their skills fill gaps in your expertise.
   Example: If you're strong in operations, a tech-savvy co-founder can balance the team.

2. ***Shared Vision***: A co-founder must align with your long-term goals.

3. ***Conflict Resolution Skills:*** Disagreements are inevitable. Choose someone who can handle conflicts constructively.

Real-Life Example

Flipkart's founders, Sachin and Binny Bansal, shared a passion for e-commerce and complemented each other's strengths. This collaboration became a key driver of their success.

When you're starting a business, one of the first decisions you'll need to make is how to legally structure it. Think of this like building a house—you need to decide on the foundation before you start building walls. Your legal structure determines how you'll pay taxes, manage liability, and even raise funds.

When I started my first business, I was clueless about these legal terms. "Sole proprietorship," "LLP," "private limited company"—it all sounded like gibberish. But once I broke it down into simple steps, things became much clearer. Let's do the same for you.

To make this easy to understand, let's imagine you want to start a chai business. You've got three options:

1. Run a small tea stall by yourself.

2. Partner with a friend who will help you run it.

3. Plan to open multiple outlets in the future with potential investors.

Now let's see which legal structure suits each scenario.

1. Sole Proprietorship: The "One-Man Army" Structure

This is the simplest form of business. You, as an individual, own and run everything. There's no separate legal identity for your business—everything is under your name.

Example: You open a chai stall in your neighbourhood. You buy supplies, serve customers, and handle profits and losses all by yourself.

Key Features:

- Super easy to start—just your PAN card and a basic registration (like Shop and Establishment License) are enough.

- Full control—you make all the decisions.

- Unlimited liability—if something goes wrong, like a customer suing you or a loan default, your personal assets (house, car) could be at risk.

Who Should Choose This?

If you're running a small-scale business, like a chai stall or freelance work, and don't plan to expand quickly, this is the best choice.

2. Partnership Firm: "Two or More Hands in the Game"

This is for businesses run by two or more people who want to share responsibilities, profits, and risks. You'll need a partnership deed—a legal document that defines who does what and how profits are shared.

Example: You and a friend decide to open a chai café together. One of you handles the kitchen, and the other handles customer service.

Key Features:

- Shared workload—you can divide tasks and responsibilities.

- Unlimited liability—just like a sole proprietorship, your personal assets are at risk.

- Disputes can arise—if your partner wants to leave or disagrees with you, it can cause trouble.

Who Should Choose This?

If you're running a small business with someone you trust and you want to share the responsibilities, a partnership is a good option.

3. Limited Liability Partnership (LLP): "Protect Yourself from Risks"

An LLP is like a partnership, but with one major advantage—your personal assets are safe. If the business owes money, only the business assets will be used to pay it off, not your personal savings or property.

Example: Your chai café is doing well, and you plan to add more branches. But you want to protect yourself from financial risks if something goes wrong. You and your partner form an LLP.

Key Features:

- Limited liability—you're not personally responsible for business debts.

- Moderate compliance—you'll need to file annual returns and maintain some records.

Who Should Choose This?

If you're scaling up your business and want legal protection for yourself, an LLP is a good choice.

4. Private Limited Company: "For Big Dreams and Investors"

This structure is perfect for startups that want to raise funds or expand quickly. A private limited company is treated as a separate legal entity—it's like your business is a person on its own.

Example: You've built a chai brand, "Desi Chai Co.," and investors want to fund you to open 50 outlets across India. To attract them, you form a private limited company.

Key Features:

- Separate legal entity—your personal and business assets are completely separate.

- Limited liability—you're protected from personal financial risks.

- Easy to raise funds—investors prefer this structure.

Who Should Choose This?

If you're planning to scale your business, raise funds, or go big, this is the best option.

5. One Person Company (OPC): "A Private Limited for Solopreneurs"

If you're a solo entrepreneur but want the benefits of a private limited company, OPC is a great choice. It's like a one-person version of a private limited company.

Example: You want to build a chai delivery app by yourself, but you need protection from financial risks. You form an OPC.

Key Features:

- Limited liability—your personal assets are safe.
- A separate legal entity—just like a private limited company.

Who Should Choose This?

If you're a solo founder with plans to grow your business and want legal protection, go for an OPC.

Beginner-Friendly Steps to Choose and Register

1. **Start Small**: If you're just starting and testing your idea, begin with a sole proprietorship.

2. **Move Up as You Grow**: If you partner with someone or scale, transition to an LLP or private limited company.

3. **Get Help**: Consult a chartered accountant or legal expert to guide you through the process.

Why Does Legal Structure Matter?

Your legal structure determines:

1. **Who's responsible for the business liabilities** (you or the company).

2. **How you pay taxes**—whether as an individual or as a business entity.

3. **How you manage ownership**—solo, with partners, or through shareholders.

4. **Your ability to raise funds**—some structures attract investors more easily.

How to Choose the Right Legal Structure

Ask yourself these questions:

1. **Am I starting alone or with a partner?**

   - If you're solo, start with a **sole proprietorship** or **One Person Company (OPC)**.

   - If you're with partners, consider a **Partnership Firm** or **Limited Liability Partnership (LLP)**.

2. **How much risk am I willing to take?**

- If you want to protect your personal assets, avoid structures like **sole proprietorship** or **partnership**, which come with **unlimited liability**. Instead, opt for **LLP** or **private limited company**.

3. **What are my growth plans?**

- For small businesses like freelancing or a chai stall, simpler structures like **sole proprietorship** are fine.
- For startups aiming to scale and raise funding, a **private limited company** is ideal.

4. **Do I need funding or investors?**

- Investors prefer structured entities like **private limited companies** because they are transparent and scalable.

Let's Break It Down: Structure Examples

Structure	Who's It For?	Liability	Complexity
Sole Proprietorship	Solo founders running small businesses.	Unlimited (high risk).	Easiest to start.
Partnership Firm	Small teams sharing workload and profits.	Unlimited (high risk).	Moderately easy.
Limited Liability Partnership	Small to medium businesses seeking protection.	Limited (safe).	Moderate compliance.
Private Limited Company	Startups planning to scale or attract investors.	Limited (safe).	High compliance.

Structure	Who's It For?	Liability	Complexity
One Person Company (OPC)	Solo founders wanting to scale with safety.	Limited (safe).	High compliance.

Step-by-Step Guide to Register Your Business

Once you've chosen the right structure, here's how to get started:

1. For Sole Proprietorship:

- **Registration**: Apply for a local Shop and Establishment License.

- **GST**: Get GST registration if your turnover exceeds ₹40 lakhs annually (₹20 lakhs for services).

- **PAN Card**: Your personal PAN card will be used for all financial activities.

Example: You start a chai stall in your area. To avoid legal trouble, you get a basic Shop Act license.

2. For Partnership Firm:

- **Partnership Deed**: Create a legal document defining each partner's roles, responsibilities, and profit-sharing ratio.

- **Registration**: Register the partnership with the Registrar of Firms (not mandatory, but advisable).

- **PAN Card**: Get a separate PAN for the partnership.

Example: You and a friend decide to start a chai café. A partnership deed ensures clarity and avoids future disputes.

3. For Limited Liability Partnership (LLP):

- **Digital Signature Certificate (DSC)**: Apply for DSCs for the designated partners.

- **LLP Registration**: File for incorporation on the Ministry of Corporate Affairs (MCA) portal.

- **Annual Compliance**: Maintain books of accounts and file annual returns.

Example: Your chai café is growing, and you want legal protection. Forming an LLP keeps your personal savings safe.

4. For Private Limited Company:

- **Name Approval**: Use the RUN (Reserve Unique Name) service on the MCA portal.

- **Company Registration**: File for incorporation with necessary documents, like the Memorandum of Association (MoA) and Articles of Association (AoA).

- **Tax Compliance**: Obtain a Corporate Identification Number (CIN) and GST registration.

Example: Your chai business expands, and investors show interest. A private limited company makes your business attractive for funding.

Real-World Inspiration:

- **Flipkart**: Began as a private limited company, which allowed them to attract global investors and scale into a billion-dollar e-commerce platform.

- **Dabbawala Service (Mumbai)**: Operates like a sole proprietorship model—simple, low-cost, and highly efficient.

Key Takeaways

1. Start with the simplest structure (like sole proprietorship) if you're testing your business idea.

2. Move to a more advanced structure (like LLP or private limited) when you scale or seek investors.

3. Always consult a legal or financial advisor to guide you through the process.

Pro Tip: Don't overcomplicate things at the start. The goal is to focus on your business idea first and refine the legal aspects as you grow.

Always think of the long-term vision for your business. Your legal structure should align with your growth plans, not just your current situation.

CHAPTER 3

CRAFTING A BUSINESS PLAN

A business without a plan is like a ship without a compass—it has no direction. As a former Merchant Navy officer, I can tell you firsthand how vital a clear course is to reach your destination. In the world of business, your **business plan** is that course.

But don't worry, you don't need a fancy MBA degree to create one! Let's break it down step by step in a way that's easy to understand and actionable.

What Is a Business Plan?

A business plan is simply a written document that outlines:

1. **What your business is about** (idea or product).

2. **Who your customers are** (target audience).

3. **How you'll make money** (revenue model).

4. **What resources you need** (money, team, tools).

5. **Your future goals** (short-term and long-term plans).

Think of it as a Google Map for your business—it shows you where you are and helps you plan how to get where you want to be.

Why Do You Need a Business Plan?

1. **Clarity**: Helps you organize your ideas and define your goals.

2. **Focus**: Keeps you and your team aligned and focused on what matters.

3. **Funding**: Investors or banks won't give you money without a solid plan.

4. **Risk Reduction**: Identifies potential challenges before they become real problems.

Example: When I started my first business, I had a simple plan scribbled in a notebook—what I wanted to sell, who I'd sell it to, and how much it would cost. It wasn't perfect, but it gave me a direction.

How to Create a Business Plan (Step-by-Step)

Let's make it easy with seven sections:

1. Executive Summary

- This is a 1-2 page overview of your entire business plan.

- It's the first thing people read but the last thing you write.

- *Include*:

  - Your business idea (e.g., "I'm starting a chai café that serves unique regional teas").

  - Your mission and vision.

  - A snapshot of your goals (e.g., "Target ₹5 lakh revenue in the first year").

2. Business Idea

- Describe **what your business is** and **why it's unique**.

- *Example:*

   "We sell chai with a twist—local flavors like masala, tulsi, and even paan chai to attract chai enthusiasts and adventurous customers."

3. Market Research

- Understand your target audience and competitors.

- Answer:

   - Who are my customers? (Age, income, preferences).

   - What are their problems?

   - Who else is solving these problems, and how can I do it better?

- *Example:*

   If you're opening a chai café in a college area, your target audience is students who need affordable, tasty chai.

- *How to Conduct Market Research:*

   1. **Surveys and Feedback**: Tools like Google Forms or Typeform can help you gather data directly from your target audience.

   2. **Competitor Research**: Visit competitors' websites, analyze their pricing, and study customer reviews to identify gaps.

   3. **Industry Reports**: Use resources like Statista, IBISWorld, or government data to understand market trends.

SWOT Analysis for Competitive Analysis:

- **Strengths**: What makes your competitors successful?

- **Weaknesses**: Where are they lacking?

- **Opportunities**: What gaps can you fill?

- **Threats**: What challenges could hinder your growth?

Example SWOT for a Food Delivery Startup:

- **Strength**: Faster delivery in a specific region.

- **Weakness**: Limited menu options.

- **Opportunity**: Growing demand for organic and healthy food.

- **Threat**: Established players like Zomato and Swiggy.

When I started researching my competitors, I read customer reviews on platforms like Amazon and Google to understand what customers loved—and where they were frustrated.

4. Marketing and Sales Strategy

- Outline how you'll attract customers and make sales.

- **Marketing**: Social media ads, word-of-mouth, promotions.

- **Sales**: Subscription plans, discounts on bulk orders, etc.

- *Example*:

  "Offer a 'Chai Lover's Card'—buy 5 chais, get the 6th free. Use Instagram reels to showcase your chai-making process."

5. Revenue Model

- How will you make money?
- Mention your pricing strategy, expected profit margins, and income streams.

Examples of Revenue Models:

1. **Subscription Model**: Customers pay regularly for access to services (e.g., Netflix).
2. **Freemium Model**: Offer free basic services and charge for premium features (e.g., Spotify).
3. **Marketplace Model**: Earn through commissions by connecting buyers and sellers (e.g., Flipkart).

6. Operations Plan

- List what you need to run your business daily:
    - Location (rented shop, food truck, or cloud kitchen).
    - Supplies (tea leaves, milk, spices).
    - Team (chai maker, cashier).
- *Example*:

    "Operate from 7 AM to 7 PM. Hire 1 chai maker and 1 helper."

7. Financial Projections

- Estimate your income, expenses, and profits for the next 6-12 months.
- Be realistic—investors like numbers backed by logic.

- ***Example**:*

  - ○ Monthly revenue: ₹60,000 (selling 3,000 cups at ₹20).

  - ○ Monthly expenses: ₹35,000 (rent, ingredients, salary).

  - ○ Profit: ₹25,000/month.

Real-Life Business Plan Example: *Chai Point*

Chai Point, one of India's biggest chai brands, started with a simple plan: bring hygienic and premium chai to urban Indians. They focused on delivery and tech-enabled kiosks, targeting office-goers who didn't have access to good chai during work hours.

Their business plan included:

1. **Target Audience**: Working professionals.

2. **Marketing Strategy**: Kiosks in IT parks, bulk orders for offices.

3. **Revenue Model**: Selling chai and snacks with high-profit margins.

Quick Business Plan Template for Beginners

If you're feeling overwhelmed, start with this simple template:

Section	Key Points
Business Idea	What are you selling? Who is your customer?
Market Research	Who are your competitors? What's your unique selling point (USP)?

Section	Key Points
Marketing Strategy	How will you attract customers?
Revenue Model	How much will you charge? What are your expenses?
Goals	Short-term: "Sell 1,000 units in 3 months." Long-term: "Expand to 3 locations in 2 years."

Checklist for Crafting a Business Plan:

- ☐ Have I defined my target audience and created a customer persona?

- ☐ Have I conducted market research using surveys, competitor analysis, and industry reports?

- ☐ Have I identified my startup's strengths, weaknesses, opportunities, and threats (SWOT)?

- ☐ Do I have a clear revenue model for my business?

- ☐ Have I calculated the break-even point to understand when I'll cover my costs?

Pro Tip for Beginners

Don't overthink or overcomplicate your plan. Write what you know, start small, and improve as you go. A rough plan that gets you started is better than a perfect plan that keeps you stuck.

CHAPTER 4

BUILDING YOUR CORE TEAM

Starting a business is exciting, but let's face it—you can't do everything alone. A strong, motivated, and skilled team can be the difference between your business thriving or struggling. In this section, let's focus on **how to identify, hire, and manage your dream team**, even if you're just starting out.

Why Is Building the Right Team So Important?

A business isn't just about a great idea—it's about execution. And execution requires people. The right team:

1. **Shares your vision** and works towards your goals.

2. Brings **skills you may lack**, like marketing, finance, or operations.

3. Helps you **stay focused** by managing day-to-day tasks.

4. **Inspires confidence** in investors and customers—they trust a strong, competent team.

Example: When I started my entrepreneurial journey after leaving the Merchant Navy, I realized quickly that I couldn't handle everything. I lacked expertise in marketing and operations. So, I hired a marketer who was great at digital outreach and someone who knew how to manage logistics.

Flipkart's early hires focused on supply chain experts who helped scale their logistics operations, making it easier to grow rapidly.

Step-by-Step Guide to Building Your Core Team

Step 1: Identify the Roles You Need

Every business needs specific roles to function. Ask yourself:

1. **What tasks can I handle myself?** (e.g., sales or product development).
2. **What tasks need expertise?** (e.g., graphic design, accounting).
3. **What roles are critical to my business?**

Here's a basic breakdown:

Role	Responsibilities
Founder/Owner	Vision, leadership, and decision-making.
Marketer	Promoting the business, running social media, attracting leads.
Operations Manager	Managing daily business operations, logistics, and inventory.

Role	Responsibilities
Finance/Accountant	Tracking income, expenses, taxes, and budgeting.
Customer Support	Handling customer queries and ensuring satisfaction.

Pro Tip: Start small. You don't need a big team initially—just focus on critical roles.

Step 2: Find the Right People

Here's how to find the best talent, even on a budget:

1. ***Leverage Your Network***:
   Ask friends, family, and former colleagues for recommendations. Sometimes, the best hires come through word of mouth.

   - ***Example***: When I needed a video editor for my content creation journey, I reached out to my network and found someone talented and affordable.

2. ***Look for Passion Over Experience***:
   Early-stage businesses benefit from passionate people willing to grow with the company. Don't stress too much over resumes.

3. ***Hire Freelancers for Specialized Tasks***:
   Platforms like **Upwork**, **Fiverr**, and **LinkedIn** are great for hiring freelancers if you can't afford full-time employees.

   - ***Example:*** A startup can hire a freelance graphic designer for ₹5,000–₹10,000 per project instead of hiring someone full-time.

4. *Interns and Freshers*:
   Interns are affordable and often bring fresh ideas. Many startups hire interns and convert the best ones into full-time employees.

Step 3: Conduct Smart Interviews

Ask questions that reveal the candidate's skills, attitude, and cultural fit. Here are a few:

1. *Skill-Based Questions*:
   - "Can you show me examples of your previous work?"
   - "How would you approach this task?" (Give a hypothetical situation).

2. *Behavioral Questions*:
   - "Tell me about a time you solved a tough problem at work."
   - "How do you handle deadlines or pressure?"

3. *Cultural Fit Questions*:
   - "What motivates you to work for a startup?"
   - "Do you enjoy learning new things?"

Step 4: Set Clear Expectations

Once you've hired the right people, make sure everyone knows their responsibilities.

1. **Create a Clear Job Description**: Mention key tasks and outcomes expected.

2. **Set SMART Goals**: Goals should be *Specific, Measurable, Achievable, Relevant, and Time-bound*.

3. **Communicate Regularly**: Use tools like *Slack, Trello*, or even WhatsApp to stay in sync.

Example*:* For a marketing role, a SMART goal could be: "Increase Instagram followers by 20% in 3 months using organic strategies."

Step 5: Creating a Team Culture

- ***Why Team Culture Matters****:*
  A strong culture fosters collaboration, innovation, and loyalty among employees.

- ***Steps to Build a Positive Culture****:*

  1. Define core values (e.g., transparency, customer-first, adaptability).

  2. Encourage open communication.

  3. Recognize and reward good performance.

Example*:* Zappos, the e-commerce company, became famous for its culture of employee happiness, leading to exceptional customer service and a loyal team.

Real-Life Examples of Team Building

1. **Flipkart:**
   Sachin and Binny Bansal started Flipkart as a two-person team. Initially, they did everything themselves—coding, packing orders, and customer support. As demand grew, they started hiring for specific roles like delivery personnel and marketers.

2. **OYO Rooms**:
   Ritesh Agarwal, the founder of OYO, relied on a lean but
   motivated team in the early days. He focused on hiring people
   passionate about redefining India's hospitality industry.

Key Takeaways for Beginners

1. **Don't rush** into hiring—identify what you truly need.

2. **Start small** and hire for critical roles first.

3. Look for people who **believe in your vision**—skills can be
   taught, but attitude matters most.

4. Use affordable options like freelancers, interns, or part-timers if
   your budget is tight.

5. Keep communicating with your team to maintain focus and
   motivation.

Checklist for Building Your Core Team:

☐ Have I identified the key roles my business needs right now?

☐ Have I leveraged my network, freelance platforms, or interns to
find talent?

☐ Have I conducted interviews focusing on skills, behavior, and
cultural fit?

☐ Have I defined my company's core values and created a positive
team culture?

☐ Do I have an onboarding plan to set new hires up for success?

CHAPTER 5

Imagine you're navigating a ship without knowing the weather or tides—it's risky, right? The same applies to starting a business without understanding your market. Market research is your radar that helps you understand your customers, competitors, and the industry landscape.

What Is Market Research and Why Is It Important?

Market research is the process of gathering and analyzing information about:

1. **Your Target Customers**: Who they are, what they need, and how they behave.

2. **Your Competitors**: What they offer, their strengths, and their weaknesses.

3. **Industry Trends**: What's happening in the market and where it's headed.

Why It Matters:

- Helps you build a product or service that **solves real problems**.

- Identifies gaps in the market that you can fill.

- Guides your **pricing, marketing, and sales strategies**.

- Minimizes risks by helping you make informed decisions.

Real Impact of Market Research:

Market research is the foundation of every successful business strategy. It helps you understand customer behavior, predict trends, and identify market gaps.

Example: When Swiggy started, they analyzed why competitors like Foodpanda were struggling. They discovered inefficiencies in delivery times and focused on building a robust delivery network to address this pain point.

Pro Tip: Market research isn't a one-time activity—it's an ongoing process. Customer needs and market conditions change, so keep researching to stay ahead.

Step-by-Step Guide to Market Research

Step 1: Define Your Target Audience

Your target audience is the group of people most likely to buy your product or service. Ask yourself:

- Who are they? (Age, gender, location, income).

- What do they want? (Needs, problems, desires).

- How do they behave? (Where do they shop, what influences their decisions).

Example:

If you're opening a chai café near a college, your target audience is likely students aged 18-25 who want affordable and tasty chai during breaks.

How to Find This Info:

- **Surveys**: Use Google Forms to ask potential customers about their preferences.

- **Interviews**: Talk to people in your target demographic.

- **Social Media**: Check what your audience engages with online.

Step 2: Analyze Your Competition

Competitors are businesses offering similar products or services. Study them to understand:

- **What they're doing well** (strengths).

- **Where they're falling short** (weaknesses).

- **How you can differentiate yourself** (your unique selling point, or USP).

How to Research Competitors:

1. Visit their website and social media.

2. Read customer reviews on Google, Amazon, or Zomato (depending on your industry).

3. Observe their pricing, marketing tactics, and customer base.

Example:

If a competitor chai café focuses only on delivery, you can differentiate by offering a cozy seating area for customers to relax.

Step 3: Study Industry Trends

Markets change constantly, and staying updated helps you adapt. Look for:

- What's trending (e.g., healthier options like sugar-free or green tea).

- Economic factors (e.g., are people spending more or saving?).

- Technology advancements (e.g., mobile apps for ordering).

How to Find Trends:

- Read industry reports on websites like **Statista** or **IBEF**.

- Follow relevant blogs, podcasts, or YouTube channels.

- Join Facebook or LinkedIn groups in your niche.

Example:

In the chai industry, the growing trend of environmentally friendly packaging (like paper cups instead of plastic) can give you a competitive edge.

Methods of Conducting Market Research:

1. **Primary Research**: Collecting firsthand information through:

   - *Surveys*: Use tools like Google Forms or Typeform to ask customers about their preferences.

   - *Interviews*: Talk directly to potential customers to understand their pain points.

- *Focus Groups*: Gather small groups to discuss your product or service.

2. **Secondary Research**: Analyzing existing data through:

   - *Industry reports* (e.g., Statista, IBISWorld).

   - *Competitor analysis* (e.g., studying reviews on Amazon or Google).

   Example: Mamaearth conducted focus groups to test their toxin-free baby products. Feedback from parents helped them refine their products before launch.

When **Zomato** started, they focused on solving a specific problem: people didn't know where to find restaurant menus online. Their market research revealed a gap in this area. They began by digitizing menus and listing restaurants, and later expanded into food delivery. Today, Zomato is a global giant because they consistently analyze market needs and adapt to trends.

Common Tools for Market Research

Here are some tools to make market research easier:

1. **Google Trends**: Understand what people are searching for online.

2. **Facebook and Instagram Insights**: Analyze your audience's behavior on social media.

3. **SurveyMonkey**: Create professional surveys to collect data.

4. **SEMrush**: Study your competitors' online presence.

5. **Quora and Reddit**: See what questions people are asking in your industry.

Pro Tip: Combine multiple tools to get a holistic view. For example, use Google Trends to identify customer interests and SurveyMonkey to validate those interests with real data.

How to Use Market Research to Your Advantage

Once you've gathered data, use it to:

1. **Improve Your Product/Service**: Make sure it solves a real problem.

2. **Refine Your Marketing**: Focus on platforms and messages that resonate with your audience.

3. **Set Competitive Pricing**: Charge based on what customers are willing to pay.

4. **Find New Opportunities**: Spot gaps in the market your competitors aren't addressing.

Pro Tip for Beginners

Don't overthink market research. Start small:

- Talk to 10-15 potential customers to get insights.

- Analyze 2-3 competitors.

- Use free tools like Google Forms and social media analytics.

The goal isn't to create a perfect research report—it's to understand your market well enough to make informed decisions.

Checklist for Understanding Market Research:

- ☐ Have I conducted primary research (e.g., surveys, interviews)?

- ☐ Have I analyzed secondary research (e.g., industry reports, competitor analysis)?

- ☐ Have I identified tools to make my research more effective (e.g., Google Trends, SEMrush)?

- ☐ Have I applied my findings to refine my product, pricing, and marketing strategies?

- ☐ Have I created a plan to continue market research regularly?

CHAPTER 6

VALIDATING YOUR BUSINESS IDEA

Starting a business is exciting, but before investing time and money, you need to ask one critical question: **Will people actually buy what I'm offering?**
This is where **idea validation** comes in—it's the process of testing whether your business idea has potential in the real world. Let's break this down into simple, actionable steps.

What is Idea Validation?

Validation is about proving that your business idea solves a real problem and that people are willing to pay for your solution. It's like testing the waters before diving in.

Example:
Imagine you're planning to sell handcrafted diaries online. Validation helps you check whether people are willing to pay ₹500 for a diary or if they'd prefer a ₹200 one from Amazon.

Why is Validation Important?

1. **Save Money**: It prevents you from investing in a product nobody wants.

2. **Save Time**: You'll focus only on ideas that show promise.

3. **Improve Your Offering**: Early feedback helps you refine your product or service.

Example:

When Zomato started, it was just a website with restaurant menus. They didn't jump straight into food delivery—they tested the waters by understanding what users wanted first.

Long-Term Impact of Validation:

Validation not only saves time and money but also builds confidence in your idea. It helps you pitch better to investors and establish credibility among stakeholders.

The founders of Urban Company validated their idea by offering basic services manually before investing in an app. This approach helped them avoid costly mistakes in development.

How to Validate Your Business Idea

1. Start with the Problem

Every successful business solves a problem. Ask yourself:

- What problem is my idea solving?

- Who has this problem?

- Is it a small inconvenience or a big pain point?

Example:

Imagine you're building a chai delivery service. The problem could be: "Busy office workers can't leave their desks to get chai during work hours."

2. Create a Minimum Viable Product (MVP)

An MVP is a simple, bare-bones version of your product or service designed to test your idea. It doesn't have to be perfect; it just has to work.

Different Types of MVPs:

1. **Landing Pages**: Create a single webpage to describe your product and measure interest through sign-ups.

   - *Example*: Dropbox used a demo video to gauge interest before building their actual product.

2. **Concierge MVP**: Offer a manual service to test demand.

   - *Example*: Airbnb began by renting out air mattresses in their own apartment during an event.

3. **Wizard of Oz MVP**: Pretend to have a fully automated system while manually completing tasks behind the scenes.

   - *Example*: Zappos started by listing shoe pictures online and buying them from stores once customers placed orders.

Choose an MVP that aligns with your product type and available resources.

MVP Examples:

- If you want to sell healthy snacks, start by selling a small batch to friends and family.

- For a mobile app idea, create a landing page describing the app and collect email sign-ups.

- If you're planning a service like social media management, take one client for free and gather feedback.

3. Talk to Potential Customers

The best way to validate your idea is by talking to people who might buy your product or service.

How to Do It:

- Conduct surveys using tools like Google Forms or Typeform.

- Talk to people in your target audience and ask open-ended questions:

    - What's the biggest challenge you face in your industry?

    - Would you pay for a solution? If yes, how much?

Example:
Mamaearth, a skincare brand, started by talking to parents about their concerns regarding baby care products. They learned that parents wanted chemical-free options, which became the foundation of their brand.

4. Use Social Media for Quick Validation

Social media platforms are powerful tools to test your idea.

Steps to Test Your Idea on Social Media:

- Create a post or ad describing your product.

- Run a small-budget ad campaign (₹500-₹1000) on Instagram or Facebook.

- Track engagement: How many people click, comment, or message you?

- Create polls on Instagram or Twitter to ask for opinions about your product.

- Share mockups or prototypes and track engagement (likes, comments, shares).

Example:

Suppose you want to launch a range of fitness apparel. Post a photo of your designs on Instagram with a poll: "Would you buy this? Yes/No." If you get a strong positive response, your idea has potential.

5. Test the Market with Landing Pages

A landing page is a one-page website where you can explain your idea and collect leads.

How to Create a Landing Page:

1. Use free tools like Wix, WordPress, or Carrd.

2. Write a catchy headline describing your product.

3. Add a clear call-to-action (e.g., "Sign Up for Early Access" or "Pre-Order Now").

4. Share the page with your network or run ads to drive traffic.

Example:

Imagine you're starting an online baking class. Create a landing page with details about your classes and collect sign-ups. If 50 people show interest, you know your idea has potential.

How to Analyze the Results

After testing, review your results:

- **Interest**: Did people show interest in your product/service?

- **Engagement**: Did people click, sign up, or buy?

- **Feedback**: What did people like or dislike about your idea?

Metrics to Evaluate Validation:

1. **Conversion Rates**: What percentage of people showed interest or signed up?

   - *Example*: If 500 people visit your landing page and 50 sign up, your conversion rate is 10%.

2. **Customer Feedback Quality**: Are customers excited about your product, or do they have major reservations?

3. **Pre-Sales or Early Purchases**: If people are willing to pay upfront, it's a strong validation signal.

If your results are positive, congratulations! You're ready to move forward. If not, don't be discouraged—use the feedback to refine your idea and try again.

Real-Life Validation Success Stories

1. **Urban Company**: They started by manually connecting customers with service providers (like plumbers and beauticians) to test demand before building their app.

2. **Nykaa**: Falguni Nayar began with a curated selection of beauty products and used customer feedback to expand her offerings.

3. **Beardo**: The men's grooming brand ran Instagram ads featuring bearded models to validate demand before launching their products.

Key Takeaway

Validation isn't about proving that your idea is perfect—it's about finding out if people care enough to pay for it. Start small, learn from feedback, and keep refining until you get it right.

Checklist for Idea Validation

- ☐ Have I identified the problem my idea solves and who it solves it for?

- ☐ Have I created a simple MVP to test my idea?

- ☐ Have I gathered feedback through surveys, interviews, or social media?

- ☐ Have I used tools like landing pages or ads to validate interest?

- ☐ Have I analyzed the data and adjusted my idea accordingly?

CHAPTER 7

SALES AND CUSTOMER ACQUISITION

Why Sales and Customer Acquisition Matter

Imagine you've built the best product in the market, but nobody buys it. Without sales and a proper strategy to acquire customers, even the most innovative startups fail. Generating revenue is the ultimate goal of every business, and your ability to acquire and retain customers determines your startup's growth and survival.

Take **Flipkart**, for example. When it launched, it was just a small online bookstore. The founders, Sachin and Binny Bansal, knew that acquiring customers in India's price-sensitive market wouldn't be easy. They focused on delivering exceptional service—cash on delivery and free delivery—which became game-changers in the Indian e-commerce space. Their ability to attract and retain customers helped them grow into the giant we know today.

Sales isn't just about closing deals; it's about understanding your customers' needs and offering them value. A solid sales strategy can turn one-time buyers into loyal advocates of your brand."

Mamaearth focused on customer relationships by actively engaging with parents in parenting groups, building trust and creating a loyal customer base.

Understanding Your Target Customer

Before you can sell, you need to understand who you're selling to. Without clarity about your target customer, you risk wasting resources on people who don't need or want your product.

Steps to Identify Your Target Customers

1. **Create a Customer Persona**: Build a fictional profile of your ideal customer, including:

   - **Demographics**: Age, gender, income, location, and profession.

   - **Psychographics**: Interests, values, and behaviors.

   - **Pain Points**: Challenges they face that your product can solve.

   Example: When Ola entered the Indian market, they focused on urban professionals who needed convenient and affordable transport. By identifying this niche, they positioned their app as a time-saving solution for city commuters.

2. **Analyze Competitors**: Study businesses in your niche to understand their target audience. What's working for them? How can you differentiate your offering?
   Example: Cred studied existing payment apps like Paytm and PhonePe but differentiated itself by targeting premium users who wanted rewards for paying credit card bills.

3. **Conduct Surveys and Interviews**: Use online tools like Google
   Forms or in-person interviews to gather insights directly from
   potential customers.

Finding Your First Customers: Early Adopters

Your early adopters are crucial—they're the first people who will use
your product, give feedback, and spread the word. Early adopters are
typically risk-takers who are open to trying new things.

Steps to Find Early Adopters

1. **Leverage Your Network**: Start by reaching out to friends, family,
   and colleagues who might be interested or know someone who
   would be.
   Example: The founders of Urban Company (formerly
   UrbanClap) reached out to friends and acquaintances to try
   their home services platform before scaling it to a broader
   audience.

2. **Attend Industry Events**: Networking events, trade shows, or
   even meetups can help you connect with potential customers
   who are already interested in your industry.
   Example: Zerodha built Its customer base by attending financial
   workshops and educating participants about low-cost stock
   trading.

3. **Online Communities**: Use platforms like Reddit, Quora, and
   Facebook Groups to connect with people who fit your target
   audience.
   Example: A D2C startup selling sustainable clothing could join

eco-conscious Facebook groups to promote their products and receive feedback.

Pro tip:

- ○ Collaborate with influencers in your niche to reach early adopters.

- ○ Offer exclusive discounts to your first 100 customers as an incentive.

Cred initially targeted premium credit card users by offering exclusive rewards, ensuring their early adopters felt valued.

Sales Strategies for Startups

1. Inbound Sales (Let Customers Come to You)

This strategy focuses on attracting potential customers to your business using marketing techniques like SEO, blogs, and social media.

Example: Nykaa built its beauty empire through strong inbound marketing. By creating tutorials, product reviews, and influencer partnerships, they attracted customers to their platform without hard selling.

How to Start:

- Build a blog around your product or service. Write content that answers common customer questions.

- Use Instagram and LinkedIn to showcase your brand and attract potential customers.

2. Outbound Sales (Actively Reach Out)

Outbound sales involve directly approaching potential customers through methods like cold emails, calls, or LinkedIn outreach.
Example: Freshworks, a Chennai-based SaaS company, started by cold-emailing businesses in the US to pitch their CRM software. Their personalized approach helped them acquire their first big clients.

How to Start:

- Create a list of potential customers.

- Send personalized cold emails explaining how your product solves their problem.

- Use tools like Apollo.io or LinkedIn Sales Navigator for prospecting.

3. Word-of-Mouth Sales

Happy customers are your best salespeople. Provide excellent service, and they'll recommend your product to others.
Example: Mamaearth used word-of-mouth marketing extensively. New moms shared their positive experiences with the baby-care brand in WhatsApp and Facebook groups, creating a ripple effect.

How to Encourage It:

- Offer referral bonuses. For example, give discounts to customers who refer others.

- Create a wow factor. Exceptional customer service or unique packaging can encourage people to talk about your brand.

- Encourage satisfied customers to leave online reviews on platforms like Google or Amazon.

Zerodha built trust through free educational content and word-of-mouth, attracting new users to their trading platform.

Building a Sales Funnel

A sales funnel maps out your customer's journey, helping you guide them from discovery to purchase.

Stages of a Sales Funnel

1. **Awareness**: Customers learn about your brand through ads, social media, or PR.
   Example: Swiggy's quirky ads on Instagram create brand awareness among food lovers.

2. **Interest**: They explore your offerings through your website, reviews, or free trials.
   Example: Netflix attracts customers by offering a free trial period, sparking interest in their service.

3. **Decision**: Customers are ready to buy. Make the process smooth by offering discounts or easy checkout options.
   Example: Amazon uses one-click ordering to simplify the purchase process.

4. **Action**: The customer makes a purchase.
   Example: D2C brands like Boat ensure fast delivery and post-purchase support to create a positive first experience.

Measuring Success in Sales and Customer Acquisition

1. Customer Acquisition Cost (CAC)

- The cost of acquiring one customer.
  Formula: Total Marketing Cost ÷ Number of Customers Acquired
  Example: If you spend ₹50,000 on ads and acquire 500 customers, your CAC is ₹100.

2. Customer Lifetime Value (CLV)

- The revenue you'll earn from one customer over their relationship with your business.
  Example: A Netflix subscriber who pays ₹500/month for 24 months has a CLV of ₹12,000.

3. Conversion Rate

- The percentage of leads that turn into paying customers.
  Example: If 1,000 people visit your website and 50 make a purchase, your conversion rate is 5%.

4. Customer Retention Rate

- **Formula:** (Number of customers at end of period - New customers during period) ÷ Customers at start of period.

  Example: If you start with 1,000 customers, gain 200, and lose 50, your retention rate is 95%.

5. Repeat Purchase Rate

- Tracks how many customers buy again.

  Example: D2C brands like Mamaearth focus on this metric to improve customer loyalty.

Case Study: Swiggy's Customer Acquisition Success

Swiggy started with a simple premise: *convenience.* They acquired their first customers in Bangalore by partnering with local restaurants and offering free delivery during their launch phase. Once they built trust, they introduced discounts and referral bonuses, driving more users to their app. Today, they serve millions of customers by focusing on reliability and user experience.

Checklist for Sales and Customer Acquisition

- ☐ Have I clearly defined my target customers?

- ☐ Have I identified early adopters and engaged with them effectively?

- ☐ Have I implemented at least one inbound and one outbound sales strategy?

- ☐ Have I mapped out my sales funnel?

- ☐ Am I tracking metrics like CAC, CLV, and conversion rates?

CHAPTER 8

BRANDING AND MARKETING STRATEGIES

In today's competitive market, branding and marketing are not optional—they're essential. A great product or service without effective branding and marketing is like a hidden treasure—valuable but undiscovered. This chapter will guide you through building a memorable brand and leveraging marketing strategies to scale your startup.

When I started branding my business, I learned that your brand isn't just your logo—it's the experience you create for your customers. The moment I aligned my brand voice with my audience's values, I saw a surge in engagement and trust.

What is Branding?

Branding is more than just a logo or tagline—it's the perception customers have about your business. It's your promise to the customer, the story you tell, and the emotions you evoke.

Key Components of a Brand

1. **Brand Identity:** Your visual elements, like the logo, color palette, typography, and design.

Example: Think of Apple's sleek design, clean typography, and minimalistic approach that scream "innovation and simplicity."

2. **Brand Personality**: The human traits associated with your brand (fun, professional, quirky, etc.).
   Example: Zomato's quirky, relatable social media content adds a fun personality to their brand.

3. **Brand Promise**: The commitment you make to your customers.
   Example: FedEx's promise is reliability—they deliver "when it absolutely, positively has to be there overnight."

4. **Brand Values**: The principles and ethics your company stands for.
   Example: Patagonia's focus on sustainability and environmental protection is central to its brand.

How to Build a Strong Brand

1. ***Define Your Why (Purpose)***
   Ask yourself: Why does your startup exist? What problem are you solving?
   Example: Nike doesn't just sell shoes—it inspires people to push their limits with "Just Do It."

2. ***Understand Your Target Audience***
   Your brand should resonate with your customers.
   Example: Sugar Cosmetics targets young, urban women by creating vibrant, bold makeup products that align with their lifestyle.

3. ***Create a Unique Value Proposition (UVP)***
   This explains why customers should choose you over competitors.
   Example: Ola differentiates itself from other ride-hailing apps

by offering a wide range of vehicle options, from bike rides to luxury cars.

4. ***Design Consistent Visuals***
   Your logo, website, and packaging should reflect your brand's essence. Use consistent fonts, colors, and design styles.
   Example*: Google's colorful, friendly design reflects its mission to make information accessible to all.

5. ***Tell Your Brand Story***
   People connect with stories, not products. Share the journey behind your startup.
   Example*: Paper Boat shares nostalgic stories of Indian childhoods, making their drinks emotionally appealing.

Creating a Personal Brand for Founders

A strong personal brand can amplify the startup's reach.

- **Steps for Founders**:

  1. Share your entrepreneurial journey on platforms like LinkedIn.

  2. Engage in industry discussions and build thought leadership.

  3. Use Twitter for quick insights and trends.

  Example: Elon Musk's personal brand has significantly contributed to Tesla's marketing.

Marketing: Your Growth Engine

Marketing is how you communicate your brand to your target audience and persuade them to buy your product or service. Let's explore effective marketing strategies.

1. Digital Marketing

The internet is where your customers are. Leverage digital platforms to reach them.

- **Social Media Marketing**: Use platforms like Instagram, LinkedIn, and Twitter to engage with your audience.
  Example: Durex's witty Instagram posts consistently go viral, keeping their brand top-of-mind.

- **Content Marketing**: Create valuable content that solves problems for your audience.
  Example: HubSpot offers free guides and tools for marketers, positioning itself as an industry leader.

- **SEO (Search Engine Optimization)**: Optimize your website to rank higher on Google.
  Example: If you search "best vegan recipes," websites like Minimalist Baker pop up because they've mastered SEO.

- **Email Marketing**: Build an email list and nurture relationships with personalized campaigns.
  Example: Zomato's fun and engaging emails keep customers returning to their app.

2. Offline Marketing

While digital marketing is essential, offline efforts can create a more personal connection.

- **Events and Trade Shows**: Host or participate in industry events to showcase your brand.
  Example: OYO Rooms started by setting up booths in colleges to promote affordable stays for students.

- **Print Advertising**: Use newspapers, magazines, and billboards to target specific demographics.
  Example: Amul's iconic billboards have been engaging audiences with topical humour for decades.

- **Guerrilla Marketing**: Use unconventional tactics to surprise and engage your audience.
  Example: Coca-Cola's "Happiness Machine" campaign gave free drinks and gifts from vending machines, creating viral buzz.

3. Performance Marketing

This involves data-driven marketing strategies where you pay for measurable results, like clicks, leads, or sales.

- **Pay-Per-Click (PPC)**: Advertise on Google or social media platforms where you pay for every click.
  Example: Startups like Lenskart use Google Ads to target people searching for eyewear.

- **Affiliate Marketing**: Collaborate with bloggers and influencers who promote your product for a commission.
  Example: Amazon's affiliate program allows content creators to earn by recommending products.

Measuring Marketing Effectiveness

Key Metrics to Track:

1. *ROI (Return on Investment):* Calculate profit from each campaign.

2. *CTR (Click-Through Rate):* Measure ad effectiveness.

3. *Engagement Rate:* Track likes, shares, and comments on social media.

4. *Conversion Rate:* Leads turned into paying customers.

   - **Tools to Use**: Google Analytics, Facebook Ads Manager, HubSpot.

Real-Life Branding Success Stories

1. Zomato

Zomato began as a restaurant discovery platform in India. To attract users, they leveraged social media with humour, relatable posts, and memes. Today, their quirky branding makes them a favourite on Instagram and Twitter, setting them apart from competitors.

2. Tesla

Tesla's branding is rooted in innovation and sustainability. Without spending much on advertising, they created a cult-like following through social media, Elon Musk's personal branding, and word-of-mouth. Their electric cars are not just vehicles—they're a statement.

3. Mamaearth

Mamaearth differentiated itself in the crowded skincare market by focusing on natural and toxin-free products. Their marketing strategies included partnerships with mom bloggers, relatable Instagram content, and customer testimonials, which resonated with their target audience.

Building Customer Trust Through Branding

Trust is the foundation of any strong brand. Here's how to build it:

1. **Be Authentic**: Stay true to your brand values. Customers can sense when you're fake.

2. **Provide Exceptional Customer Service**: Respond promptly to queries and resolve complaints.
   Example: Amazon's hassle-free returns policy builds trust.

3. **Leverage Reviews and Testimonials**: Social proof makes your brand credible.
   Example: Cred displays customer reviews prominently on their app to build trust.

4. **Deliver Consistently**: Whether it's product quality or delivery times, consistency matters.
   Example: Domino's "30 minutes or free" promise built their reputation for fast delivery.

Final Thoughts

Branding and marketing are long-term investments, but they're worth every effort. A strong brand can create loyal customers, and effective marketing can bring them to your doorstep. Whether you're crafting a quirky social media presence like Zomato or building trust like Amazon, remember that your brand is what people say about you when you're not in the room.

Checklist for Branding and Marketing Strategies

☐ Have I defined my brand's mission, vision, and values?

☐ Is my brand identity (logo, color palette, typography) consistent across platforms?

☐ Am I using digital marketing strategies tailored to my audience?

☐ Do I have a plan for offline and performance marketing?

☐ Am I tracking key metrics like ROI, CTR, and engagement rates?

CHAPTER 9

RAISING FUND FOR YOUR STARTUP

Starting a business is thrilling, but let's face it—money is what fuels your vision. Without adequate funding, even the best ideas can fizzle out. Securing funds is one of the most crucial steps in building a startup, but it's also one of the most challenging. This chapter will walk you through different types of funding, how to choose the right option, and how to approach investors with confidence.

Why is Funding Important for Startups?

Funding allows startups to:

1. **Launch their product or service**: From initial development to marketing, capital is needed for execution.

2. **Scale operations**: Whether it's hiring more team members, increasing production, or entering new markets, growth requires resources.

3. **Stay competitive**: In industries where competition is fierce, funding helps startups invest in technology, branding, and customer acquisition to stay ahead.

Real-Life Example:
When Flipkart launched, they started small, focusing only on books. With initial funding from Accel Partners, they expanded their product categories and invested in logistics to become the e-commerce giant of India.

Types of Startup Funding

Funding isn't one-size-fits-all. There are various ways to raise capital, depending on your startup's stage, goals, and resources. Here's a breakdown of the most common types:

1. Bootstrapping (Self-Funding)

Bootstrapping means funding your business using your own savings or revenue generated from the business.

How it Works:

- Use your personal savings or reinvest profits from the business to grow organically.
- Focus on lean operations to minimize costs.

Pros:

- Full ownership and control.
- No pressure from external investors to deliver quick returns.
- Encourages discipline and cost efficiency.

Cons:

- Limited resources can restrict growth.
- High personal financial risk.

Example*:*

Zoho Corporation, a SaaS giant, has remained bootstrapped since its inception. By focusing on sustainable growth and profitability, they've avoided external funding and maintained complete independence.

When to Consider Bootstrapping:

- If your startup doesn't require heavy upfront investments.
- If you want full control over your business.

2. *Family and Friends*

Borrowing money or raising funds from people in your personal network.

How it Works:

- Approach family members, friends, or acquaintances who believe in you and your vision.
- Agree on terms—whether it's a loan or equity stake.

Pros:

- Easier to secure compared to institutional funding.
- Minimal paperwork or formalities.

Cons:

- Mixing personal relationships with money can lead to conflicts.
- The amount raised may still be limited.

Example:

Many startups, like Mamaearth, relied on family and friends for their initial funding before scaling with angel investments.

When to Consider Family and Friends:

- If you're in the early stages and need a small amount to get started.

3. Angel Investors

Angel investors are high-net-worth individuals who provide capital to startups in exchange for equity or convertible debt.

How it Works:

- Angels typically invest during the seed or early stages of a startup.

- Apart from money, they often provide mentorship and valuable connections.

Pros:

- Quick access to funds.

- Access to mentorship and industry expertise.

Cons:

- You'll need to give up a portion of your equity.

- Angels may expect higher returns or exert influence on decisions.

Example:
Oyo Rooms raised seed funding from angel investors like Manish Sinha and Bejul Somaia, which helped them refine their business model.

When to Consider Angel Investors:

- When you need funding to develop your product or scale operations.

4. Venture Capital (VC)

Venture capitalists are professional investors or firms that invest in high-growth startups in exchange for equity.

How it Works:

- VCs typically invest in startups with proven traction and scalability potential.

- They provide large funding rounds and often join the company's board to influence decisions.

Pros:

- Access to significant capital for rapid scaling.

- Networking and mentorship from experienced VCs.

Cons:

- VCs require equity and decision-making power.

- Heavy pressure to achieve high growth quickly.

Example:
Byju's raised significant VC funding from Sequoia Capital, which enabled them to expand globally and acquire smaller edtech companies.

When to Consider Venture Capital:

- When your startup has traction and needs funds to scale rapidly.

5. Bank Loans and Debt Financing

Borrowing money from banks or financial institutions with the promise to repay it with interest.

How it Works:

- Loans are typically secured against collateral or personal guarantees.
- You repay the principal and interest over time.

Pros:

- You retain full ownership of the company.
- Predictable repayment terms.

Cons:

- Interest payments can be burdensome for early-stage startups.
- Requires good credit history and collateral.

  Example:
  Many small businesses in India rely on loans from public sector banks like SBI to fund initial operations.

When to Consider Bank Loans:

- If you need funds for specific projects or equipment and have a predictable revenue stream.

6. Crowdfunding

Raising small amounts of money from a large number of people, usually via online platforms like Kickstarter, Indiegogo, or Milaap.

How it Works:

- Create a campaign showcasing your idea and goals.

- People contribute money in exchange for rewards, equity, or simply to support you.

Pros:

- Great for validating your idea and building a community.

- No need to give up equity (in reward-based crowdfunding).

Cons:

- Requires significant effort to run a successful campaign.

- Crowdfunding may not work for all industries.

Example:
Pebble, a smartwatch startup, raised $10 million on Kickstarter, proving the viability of crowdfunding for innovative tech products.

When to Consider Crowdfunding:

- If you have a unique product idea with mass appeal.

How to Run a Crowdfunding Campaign:

1. Create a compelling pitch video.

2. Offer unique rewards to backers.

3. Promote the campaign aggressively on social media.

7. Revenue-Based Financing

Borrowing capital in exchange for a fixed percentage of your future revenues until the agreed repayment amount is met. This is a flexible funding model for startups with consistent revenue streams.

How It Works

- Startups receive upfront funding based on current and projected revenues.

- Repayments are tied to monthly revenue—e.g., 5-10% of revenue—until the repayment cap is reached (usually 1.5x-2x the funding amount).

- There are no fixed timelines; repayment speeds up or slows down based on revenue performance.

Pros

- **No Equity Dilution**: Founders retain 100% ownership of their company.

- **Flexible Repayments**: Payments adjust to revenue flow, reducing financial stress during slow months.

- **Quick Access to Funds**: Faster approvals compared to equity funding or loans.

- **No Collateral Required**: Ideal for asset-light startups without significant physical assets.

Cons

- **Higher Total Cost**: The repayment cap (e.g., 1.5x-2x the funding) can result in higher costs than traditional loans.

- **Limited Applicability**: Startups with unpredictable or seasonal revenues may find it unsuitable.

- **Revenue Dependency**: Slower revenue growth can extend repayment periods and delay access to additional funds.

Example

Klub Supporting D2C Brands

- A premium skincare startup raised ₹50 lakhs through Klub to fund inventory and marketing.

- The company repaid the amount by sharing 8% of monthly revenue until they reached the repayment cap of ₹75 lakhs (1.5x the funding).

- This model allowed the brand to scale without sacrificing ownership or taking on fixed EMIs.

When to Consider Revenue-Based Financing

- If your startup generates consistent monthly revenue (e.g., ₹2-5 lakhs or more).

- When you need funding for revenue-driven activities like marketing or inventory.

- If you want to scale without diluting equity or offering collateral.

- If your business model has predictable cash flow, such as D2C, SaaS, or subscription-based services.

8. Government Grants and Subsidies

Non-repayable funds or financial incentives provided by government bodies to promote entrepreneurship, innovation, and economic growth. These are ideal for startups in sectors like technology, agriculture, healthcare, and education.

How It Works

- Governments offer grants or subsidies for specific purposes, such as research and development, skill training, or promoting women entrepreneurs.

- Startups must apply through official programs, submit proposals, and meet eligibility criteria.

- Grants do not require repayment, but the funds must be used as stipulated by the program.

Pros

- **No Repayment or Equity Dilution**: Grants and subsidies are non-repayable, allowing startups to retain full ownership.

- **Encourages Innovation**: Focused on encouraging groundbreaking ideas and solving societal problems.

- **Boosts Credibility**: Winning a government grant adds credibility and can attract investors.

Cons

- **Competitive and Lengthy Process**: Applications are competitive, and approval can take months.

- **Usage Restrictions**: Funds must be used for the specific purpose outlined in the grant proposal.

- **Documentation Requirements**: Extensive paperwork and audits are often necessary to qualify and comply.

Example

Startup India Initiative

- An Indian agritech startup secured ₹50 lakhs under the Startup India Seed Fund Scheme to develop AI-driven farming solutions.

- The funds were used to create prototypes and conduct on-field trials, significantly reducing their time to market.

When to Consider Government Grants and Subsidies

- If your startup aligns with government priorities (e.g., clean energy, skill development, or social impact).

- If you need funds for R&D, technology innovation, or capacity building.

- If you're a women-led startup or belong to sectors like healthcare, education, or agritech.

Choosing the Right Funding Option

The type of funding you choose depends on factors like your startup stage, industry, and growth goals. Here's a quick guide:

Stage	Funding Type
Idea/Prototype Stage	Bootstrapping, Family and Friends, Crowdfunding
Early Traction Stage	Angel Investors, Seed Funding
Growth Stage	Venture Capital, Bank Loans, Revenue-based, Govt. grants and subsidies
Mature Stage	Private Equity, IPO

Tips for Raising Funds Successfully

1. **Build a Strong Business Plan**: Highlight your vision, market opportunity, and financial projections.

2. **Focus on Traction**: Demonstrate early success, such as customer acquisition or revenue growth.

3. **Prepare for Rejections**: Not every investor will say yes. Learn from feedback and improve your pitch.

4. **Network Strategically**: Attend events, join entrepreneurial communities, and build relationships with potential investors.

Stages Of Startup Funding

Seed Funding: The First Step to Growth

Seed funding is the initial capital a startup raises to turn an idea into a viable product. It's often called the "seed stage" because it's like planting the first seed to grow your business. This funding helps cover essential costs like product development, hiring, and initial marketing efforts.

Sources of Seed Funding:

1. **Angel Investors**: High-net-worth individuals who invest early in startups in exchange for equity.

   - ***Example***: Ratan Tata has invested in several Indian startups like Ola and Paytm during their seed stage.

2. **Seed Funds**: Specialized venture capital firms that focus on seed-stage startups.

- *Example*: India-based Blume Ventures often invests in startups during their seed stage.

3. **Incubators and Accelerators**: Organizations that provide funding, mentorship, and resources in exchange for equity.

   - *Example*: Y Combinator helped startups like Airbnb and Dropbox during their seed phase.

How Much is Typically Raised in Seed Funding?

Seed funding rounds are usually smaller, ranging from ₹10 lakhs to ₹5 crores, depending on the startup's needs and the industry.

What Seed Investors Look For:

- A strong founding team.

- A validated idea with early traction or a minimum viable product (MVP).

- A clear market opportunity.

Series Funding: Scaling the Business

As startups grow, they raise money in different stages called **Series A, B, C, etc.**, to scale operations, expand markets, or develop new products.

1. Series A Funding: Scaling the Core Business

Series A is the first significant round of institutional funding. It typically occurs after the startup has demonstrated some traction, such as consistent revenue, a growing customer base, or strong user engagement.

Purpose:

- Scaling operations.

- Expanding the team.

- Refining the business model.

How Much is Raised?
Series A funding in India typically ranges from ₹10 crores to ₹100 crores.

Example:
Razorpay, a fintech company, raised $9 million in its Series A funding to expand its payment solutions and improve technology.

2. Series B Funding: Accelerating Growth
Series B funding focuses on accelerating growth after the company has proven its business model. It's about scaling operations, entering new markets, and building a competitive edge.

Purpose:

- Expanding product lines or offerings.

- Investing in advanced technology.

- Launching aggressive marketing campaigns.

How Much is Raised?
Series B rounds often raise between ₹50 crores to ₹500 crores, depending on the industry.

Example:
Byju's raised $75 million in Series B funding to expand its edtech platform and invest in mobile-based learning solutions.

3. Series C Funding and Beyond: Dominating the Market
Series C and subsequent funding rounds focus on market domination,

entering international markets, or preparing for a potential exit like an IPO or acquisition.

Purpose:

- Acquiring competitors or smaller companies.

- Entering global markets.

- Preparing for an IPO or other exit strategies.

How Much is Raised?
Series C rounds often raise ₹100 crores to ₹1,000 crores or more.

Example:
Swiggy raised $1 billion in its Series G round, focusing on expanding its food delivery network and introducing new verticals like Swiggy Instamart.

Key Differences Between Seed Funding and Series Funding

Aspect	Seed Funding	Series Funding (A, B, C, etc.)
Stage	Early-stage startups (idea/prototype phase).	Growth-stage startups (scaling operations).
Purpose	Build the product, validate the idea.	Scale operations, expand markets, build technology.
Investors	Angel investors, incubators, seed funds.	Venture capital firms, private equity funds.

Aspect	Seed Funding	Series Funding (A, B, C, etc.)
Amount Raised	₹10 lakhs to ₹5 crores.	₹10 crores to ₹1,000+ crores (varies by round).

Tips for Navigating Seed and Series Funding

1. **Build Traction Early**: Investors want proof that your product works. Focus on acquiring users and generating revenue before seeking funding.

2. **Pitch Progress, Not Just Potential**: Show how far you've come (e.g., customers acquired, revenue generated) rather than just presenting future plans.

3. **Maintain a Cap Table**: Keep track of how much equity you're giving away in each round to avoid losing too much control.

Common Pitfalls in Fundraising

1. Over-diluting equity early on.

2. Focusing too much on funding instead of building traction.

3. Underestimating the time required to close a deal.

- *Example*: A fintech startup struggled after giving up 40% equity in its seed round, leaving little for future investors.

Real-Life Example of Funding Rounds: Nykaa

1. **Seed Funding**: Nykaa raised ₹20 crores in its seed round from angel investors to launch its e-commerce platform.

2. **Series A**: They raised ₹60 crores in Series A to scale operations and expand their beauty product catalog.

3. **Series B and Beyond**: Nykaa raised ₹166 crores in Series D, focusing on launching private-label brands and entering physical retail.

4. **IPO**: In 2021, Nykaa went public with a valuation of over $13 billion, making it one of India's most successful startup stories.

Checklist for Choosing the Right Funding Option

☐ Have I identified my startup's stage (idea, growth, scaling)?

☐ Do I understand the pros and cons of each funding type?

☐ Have I validated my idea with early traction or customer feedback?

☐ Is my pitch deck ready with clear financial projections?

Conclusion

Funding is not just about money; it's about finding the right partners who believe in your vision and can support your growth journey. Whether you're raising seed capital to launch your product or a Series B round to expand globally, remember to stay true to your vision, be transparent with your investors, and focus on sustainable growth.

CHAPTER 10

LEGAL AND OPERATIONAL FRAMEWORK

Every successful startup is built on a solid legal and operational foundation. Ignoring these aspects can lead to fines, legal disputes, or even the shutdown of your business. This chapter will guide you through business compliance, managing taxes, financial audits, contracts, and agreements, ensuring that your startup runs smoothly and stays protected.

1. Understanding Business Compliance

Compliance refers to following the laws and regulations required to operate your business legally. These vary based on your industry, location, and business structure.

Key Areas of Compliance

1. **Business Registration:**

   - Your business must be registered under the appropriate structure (e.g., sole proprietorship, LLP, private limited company).

- o *Example*: In India, a private limited company must be registered with the Ministry of Corporate Affairs (MCA).

2. **GST and Tax Registration**:

   - o Register for GST if your business turnover exceeds ₹40 lakhs (₹20 lakhs for services).

   - o *Example*: An e-commerce business like Flipkart must register for GST to collect and pay taxes.

3. **Industry-Specific Licenses**:

   - o Certain industries require additional licenses.

   - o *Example*: Food businesses need an FSSAI license, while finance-related startups may need SEBI or RBI approvals.

4. **Employee Compliance**:

   - o If you hire employees, comply with labour laws like provident fund (PF), Employee State Insurance (ESI), and professional tax.

   - o *Example*: Zomato complies with labour laws for its delivery partners by providing insurance coverage.

2. Managing Taxes and Financial Audits

Taxation and audits are crucial for financial health and legal compliance. Mishandling taxes or skipping audits can result in penalties.

Types of Taxes for Startups

1. **Income Tax**:

   - Businesses pay income tax on profits earned. In India, startups registered under the Startup India initiative can avail of a 3-year tax holiday.

   - *Example*: A tech startup making ₹50 lakhs in annual profit must file income tax returns and pay taxes accordingly.

2. **Goods and Services Tax (GST)**:

   - Applicable to businesses selling goods or services. Ensure you collect and remit GST monthly or quarterly.

3. **TDS (Tax Deducted at Source)**:

   - If you're paying contractors or employees, you may need to deduct TDS and deposit it with the government.

Step-by-Step Guide to Filing GST and TDS

- **Filing GST**:

  1. Log in to the GST portal.

  2. Prepare GSTR-1 for sales and GSTR-3B for overall tax summary.

  3. Submit details and make the payment online.

- **Filing TDS**:

  1. Deduct the required percentage while paying vendors/employees.

  2. File TDS returns quarterly through the NSDL portal.

3. Issue Form 16 to employees or contractors.

Financial Audits

Audits verify the accuracy of your financial statements and ensure compliance with regulations.

Who Needs an Audit?

- All private limited companies and LLPs with turnover above ₹40 lakhs or capital contributions above ₹25 lakhs.

Benefits of an Audit:

- Identifies errors in financial records.
- Helps secure investor confidence.
- Ensures compliance with tax laws.

Pro Tip: Use accounting software like Zoho Books or QuickBooks to maintain accurate financial records and simplify audits.

3. Contracts and Agreements

Strong contracts protect your business from legal disputes and misunderstandings. They clearly define the roles, responsibilities, and expectations of all parties involved.

Essential Contracts for Startups

1. **Founders' Agreement**:
   - Outlines roles, responsibilities, and equity distribution among co-founders.
   - **Why it's important**: Prevents conflicts over decision-making or ownership.

- *Example:* If one founder decides to leave, the agreement specifies how their shares will be handled.

2. Employment Contracts:

- Clearly define job roles, salaries, benefits, and confidentiality obligations.

3. Non-Disclosure Agreements (NDAs):

- Protect sensitive business information from being shared or misused.

- *Example:* Startups working with freelancers or vendors often require NDAs to safeguard intellectual property.

4. Vendor and Supplier Agreements:

- Outline terms for payments, deliveries, and service levels.

- *Example:* A food delivery startup like Swiggy signs contracts with restaurants to ensure consistent food quality and delivery timelines.

5. Customer Agreements:

- For service-based startups, include terms and conditions, refund policies, and liability clauses.

6. E-Contracts

- Startups often work with remote teams or international clients, making e-contracts essential.

- **What Are E-Contracts?** Legally binding agreements signed electronically.

- **When to Use E-Contracts:** Freelancer agreements, vendor deals, NDAs.

- **Tools for E-Signatures**: DocuSign, Adobe Sign, HelloSign.
- **Legal Validity in India**: Governed by the Information Technology Act, 2000.

4. Protecting Your Startup from Legal Risks

Intellectual Property (IP) Protection

Protecting your brand, product, or technology ensures others can't copy or misuse them.

1. **Trademarks**:
   - Protects your brand name, logo, and tagline.
   - **Example**: The iconic "tick" logo of Nike is trademarked.
2. **Patents**:
   - Protects unique inventions or technology.
   - **Example**: Paytm holds patents for its QR code payment technology.
3. **Copyrights**:
   - Protects creative content like videos, blogs, or designs.
4. **Trade Secrets**:
   - Protects proprietary processes, formulas, or data.
   - **Example**: Coca-Cola's recipe is a well-guarded trade secret.

Data Privacy and Cybersecurity

In today's digital-first world, startups handle sensitive customer data. Failure to secure this data can lead to legal and reputational risks.

- **Importance of Data Privacy**: Compliance with data protection laws like GDPR (Europe), CCPA (California), or India's Personal Data Protection Bill.

- **How to Protect Data**:

  - Implement cybersecurity measures like firewalls and encryption.

  - Conduct regular security audits and staff training.

  - Use secure payment gateways (e.g., Razorpay, PayPal).

- *Example*: Paytm ensures compliance with India's data protection laws by encrypting payment data to safeguard customer transactions.

Avoiding Common Legal Mistakes

1. **Skipping Documentation**: Always formalize agreements in writing.

2. **Ignoring Compliance**: Failing to file taxes, renew licenses, or adhere to labor laws can result in penalties.

3. **Copying Content**: Using unlicensed content (like images or music) can lead to copyright claims.

4. **Not Consulting Professionals**: Always work with a legal or tax consultant to ensure compliance.

Real-Life Example: Legal Frameworks in Action

Case Study: Ola Cabs

When Ola expanded into international markets like Australia, they had to navigate complex regulatory frameworks in each country. This included compliance with local taxi laws, labour laws for drivers, and data protection laws. Their ability to adapt to different legal environments has been a key factor in their global success.

Checklist: Building a Strong Legal and Operational Framework

1. **Register Your Business**: Choose the appropriate legal structure and complete the registration process.

2. **Obtain Necessary Licenses**: Check for industry-specific licenses.

3. **Comply with Taxes**: Register for GST, TDS, and other applicable taxes.

4. **Maintain Financial Records**: Use accounting software and prepare for audits.

5. **Draft Contracts**: Have agreements for founders, employees, vendors, and customers.

6. **Protect Intellectual Property**: Trademark your brand name, logo, and any unique products or technologies.

7. **Consult Professionals**: Work with a CA or legal advisor to avoid costly mistakes.

Conclusion

Building a solid legal and operational foundation isn't glamorous, but it's critical to your startup's success. By staying compliant, protecting your intellectual property, and maintaining proper documentation, you ensure your business operates smoothly and avoids costly legal disputes. Remember, the effort you invest in getting these aspects right will save you from headaches down the road.

CHAPTER 11

SCALING YOUR STARTUP

Starting a business is challenging, but scaling it is an entirely different ballgame. Scaling isn't just about growth; it's about sustainable, efficient growth. It's about taking what works and expanding it without breaking your operations, burning out your team, or losing focus on your core goals. In this chapter, we'll cover the key strategies and steps to scale your startup effectively.

What Does Scaling Mean?

Scaling means increasing your business's capacity to grow revenue and serve more customers without significantly increasing costs or resources. It's about multiplying results while keeping operations efficient.

Example:
When **Swiggy** started, it operated in just one city—Bangalore. As demand grew, they scaled their operations to include multiple cities, hired more delivery partners, and optimized their tech platform to handle higher order volumes seamlessly.

1. Hiring and Building a Strong Team

Your team is the backbone of your startup, and as you scale, you'll need to grow your workforce strategically.

How to Hire the Right People

1. **Hire for Values, Not Just Skills**: Look for people who align with your company's mission and culture.

   - *Example*: At **Zappos**, the company is known for prioritizing cultural fit during hiring, ensuring long-term alignment.

2. **Focus on Specialists**: In the early stages, you may hire generalists who wear multiple hats. When scaling, you'll need specialists for roles like marketing, tech development, and operations.

3. **Build a Leadership Team**: As the founder, you can't manage everything. Hire experienced leaders who can take ownership of specific functions like sales, HR, and technology.

   - *Example*: Flipkart's success can be attributed to its strong leadership team, including specialists in logistics, customer service, and marketing.

Retaining Talent

- Offer competitive salaries and benefits.

- Provide growth opportunities and invest in training.

- Foster a positive work culture where employees feel valued.

2. Automating and Streamlining Operations

As you scale, manual processes that worked initially may no longer be efficient. Automation helps you save time, reduce errors, and improve productivity.

Areas to Automate

1. **Customer Support**:

   - Use chatbots and AI tools like **Freshdesk** or **Zendesk** to handle basic customer queries.

   - *Example:* Myntra uses AI-powered chat support to resolve common customer issues quickly.

2. **Marketing Automation**:

   - Tools like **HubSpot**, **Mailchimp**, or **Zoho CRM** can help automate email campaigns, lead tracking, and social media scheduling.

3. **Inventory Management**:

   - If you're in e-commerce or retail, tools like **Unicommerce** or **TradeGecko** can automate inventory tracking and restocking.

   - *Example:* Amazon's advanced inventory systems ensure products are always available across multiple warehouses.

4. **Financial Management**:

   - Automate invoicing, expense tracking, and tax filing with tools like **QuickBooks** or **Tally**.

5. **Customer Relationship Management (CRM)**

   - Tools like Salesforce or Zoho CRM centralize customer data for better decision-making.

6. **HR Automation**

   - Tools like Darwinbox or BambooHR streamline payroll, recruitment, and performance tracking.

3. Expanding into New Markets

Scaling often involves entering new geographic locations or customer segments. However, it's essential to approach expansion strategically.

Steps to Expand Successfully

1. **Research the Market**:

    - Study the new market's customer preferences, buying behavior, and competition.

    - ***Example***: When **Ola** entered international markets like Australia and the UK, they adapted their services to meet local needs, such as including high-end vehicles.

2. **Test the Market First**:

    - Start with a small pilot launch to test demand and gather feedback.

    - ***Example***: Zomato tested its food delivery services in select Indian cities before scaling nationwide.

3. **Build Local Partnerships**:

    - Collaborate with local businesses, suppliers, or influencers to establish a presence.

    - ***Example:*** Airbnb worked closely with local hosts and tourism boards when expanding globally.

4. **Adapt to Local Culture and Laws**:

    - Ensure compliance with regional regulations and tailor your marketing strategies to resonate with local audiences.

4. Managing Cash Flow During Scaling

Scaling requires significant financial resources, and managing cash flow becomes critical.

Key Tips for Managing Cash Flow

1. **Monitor Metrics**: Keep an eye on your **burn rate** (how quickly you're spending money) and ensure your runway (how long your funds will last) is sufficient.

2. **Prioritize Investments**: Focus on areas that drive growth, such as technology, marketing, and hiring.

3. **Raise Funds if Needed**: If scaling requires more capital, consider raising a Series A or B funding round.

   - *Example:* Byju's raised $150 million during its growth phase to invest in international expansion and product development.

5. Scaling Customer Acquisition

Acquiring more customers is a key part of scaling, but it should be done cost-effectively.

Strategies for Scalable Customer Acquisition

1. **Referral Programs**:

   - Encourage existing customers to bring in new ones by offering incentives.

   - *Example*: Paytm grew rapidly by rewarding users for referring friends.

2. **Content Marketing at Scale**:

   - Invest in blog posts, videos, and webinars that provide value to your audience.

   - *Example*: Zerodha's Varsity platform offers free financial education, attracting a massive user base.

3. **Paid Advertising with ROI Focus**:

   - Scale your advertising campaigns while monitoring return on investment (ROI). Use tools like Google Ads or Facebook Ads Manager to target the right audience.

4. **Partnerships and Collaborations**:

   - Partner with complementary brands to cross-promote products.

   - *Example*: Swiggy partnered with cloud kitchens to increase food delivery options for customers.

6. Avoiding Common Scaling Pitfalls

Scaling too quickly or without proper planning can lead to failures. Here's what to watch out for:

1. **Overextending Resources**:

   - Expanding too fast can strain your team, finances, and infrastructure. Scale gradually.

2. **Losing Focus**:

   - Stick to your core product or service. Avoid diversifying too early.

   - *Example:* Snapdeal lost market share when it tried to replicate Amazon's broad strategy instead of focusing on its niche.

3. **Ignoring Customer Experience**:

    o   As you scale, maintaining quality service is critical to retain customers.

Building Resilience While Scaling

o   **Invest in Redundancy**: Build buffer inventory or have backup suppliers to avoid disruptions.

o   **Strengthen IT Infrastructure**: Invest in cloud hosting (e.g., AWS) to handle traffic surges.

o   **Plan for Economic Fluctuations**: Reserve funds for unexpected slowdowns.

Real-Life Case Study: Scaling Done Right- Nykaa

Nykaa started as an online beauty retailer and scaled into a multi-channel brand with physical stores, private-label products, and a wide product portfolio. Here's how they scaled successfully:

1. Focused on their niche (beauty and wellness) before diversifying.

2. Used customer insights to expand into private-label brands.

3. Scaled customer acquisition by investing in influencer marketing and regional content.

4. Gradually expanded from e-commerce to physical stores.

Checklist for Scaling Your Startup

1. **Build a Strong Team**: Hire specialists and develop leaders.

2. **Automate Operations**: Streamline repetitive tasks using technology.

3. **Expand Thoughtfully**: Test new markets before full-scale expansion.

4. **Secure Financial Resources**: Monitor cash flow and raise funds if needed.

5. **Scale Customer Acquisition**: Use cost-effective strategies like referral programs and partnerships.

Conclusion

Scaling is one of the most exciting yet challenging phases of entrepreneurship. It requires careful planning, strategic hiring, automation, and a focus on customer acquisition. By taking calculated steps and avoiding common pitfalls, you can scale your startup sustainably and achieve long-term success.

CHAPTER 12

EXIT STRATEGIES

While starting and scaling a business is exciting, planning an exit strategy is equally important. An exit strategy defines how you, as a founder, will eventually leave or transition your role in the business while ensuring its sustainability. Whether you want to sell your company, go public, or pass it on, having a clear exit plan ensures you maximize the value of your hard work and leave your business in capable hands.

What is an Exit Strategy?

An exit strategy is a plan that outlines how the founder or investors will exit the business and realize returns on their investment. It's not about abandoning the business; it's about transitioning ownership or leadership in a way that benefits everyone involved—founders, investors, employees, and customers.

Why Do Startups Need an Exit Strategy?

1. **Maximize Returns**: Exiting at the right time allows you to cash in on the value you've created.

Example: Flipkart's founders exited after Walmart acquired the company for $16 billion, giving them significant financial returns.

2. **Attract Investors**: Investors want to know how they'll get their money back. A well-thought-out exit strategy makes your startup more appealing.

3. **Future Planning**: It allows you to prepare for leadership transitions, ensuring your business continues to thrive.

4. **Reduce Risks**: An exit strategy provides a fallback plan in case of unexpected challenges, such as market downturns or personal reasons.

Types of Exit Strategies

Here are the most common types of exit strategies for startups:

1. Acquisition: Selling Your Business

An acquisition involves selling your startup to another company. This is one of the most popular exit strategies, especially for tech startups.

How it Works:

- The acquiring company buys your business, its assets, or shares.
- You may stay involved for a transition period or exit immediately, depending on the agreement.

Advantages:

- Provides a quick and often lucrative exit.
- The acquiring company may have resources to scale your idea further.

Challenges:

- Negotiating the deal can be time-consuming.

- The acquirer may not always align with your vision.

Example:
Walmart acquired Flipkart in 2018 for $16 billion, marking the largest e-commerce acquisition in India. This exit allowed Flipkart's investors and founders to realize massive returns.

2. Initial Public Offering (IPO)

An IPO involves listing your company on a stock exchange and selling shares to the public.

How it Works:

- You go through a rigorous process of financial audits, regulatory compliance, and valuations.

- Once listed, investors and the public can buy shares of your company.

Advantages:

- Provides significant capital for future growth.

- Increases brand visibility and credibility.

Challenges:

- The process is expensive and time-consuming.

- Public companies face intense scrutiny and reporting requirements.

Example:
Nykaa went public in 2021, raising ₹5,352 crores during its IPO.

The listing turned its founder, Falguni Nayar, into one of India's richest self-made women.

3. Management Buyout (MBO)

In an MBO, the existing management team purchases the company from the founder or investors.

How it Works:

- The management team raises funds through loans or investors to buy out the company.
- The founder transitions ownership to the management team.

Advantages:

- Ensures continuity, as the business is run by people familiar with it.
- The founder can exit without disrupting operations.

Challenges:

- The management team may face financial challenges raising the required capital.

  Example:
  Many small and medium-sized businesses in India use MBOs as a smooth transition strategy when founders retire.

4. Strategic Mergers

A merger involves combining your startup with another company to create a larger, more competitive entity.

How it Works:

- Both companies pool their resources, customers, and expertise.

- Ownership and leadership are typically shared between the two entities.

Advantages:

- Combines resources to achieve faster growth.

- Offers founders a partial exit while staying involved.

Challenges:

- Requires strong alignment between the two companies' cultures and goals.

Example:
When Ola acquired Foodpanda India, it merged the food delivery business into its ecosystem to expand its service portfolio.

5. Liquidation

Liquidation involves shutting down the business and selling its assets. This is usually the last resort when other exit options aren't viable.

How it Works:

- The company sells its physical and intellectual assets, such as equipment, inventory, or patents.

- The proceeds are used to pay off debts, and any remaining amount is distributed to shareholders.

Advantages:

- A quick and straightforward process.

- Allows founders to exit with some financial returns.

Challenges:

- Returns are usually lower than other exit strategies.

- It can negatively impact employees and customers.

Example:
Startups like Stayzilla, which struggled to compete, opted for liquidation when no other viable exit options were available.

6. Secondary Sales

Secondary sales, where investors sell their shares to other investors without exiting the company entirely, is a common partial exit strategy in startups.

How It Works:

- Early-stage investors sell part of their shares to later-stage investors.
- Founders may also liquidate some equity for personal financial planning.

Advantages:

- Provides liquidity to founders and early investors without giving up control.
- Brings in strategic investors who can help scale the business.

Example:

- Ola's early investors sold part of their equity to Temasek during a later funding round, ensuring liquidity without diluting founder control.

How to Prepare for an Exit Strategy

1. Build a Valuable Business

- Focus on creating a strong brand, loyal customers, and sustainable revenue.

- A company with recurring revenue, a unique product, and a solid team is more attractive to buyers or investors.

2. Keep Financial Records Clean

- Maintain accurate and transparent financial statements.

- Investors and acquirers will scrutinize your financial history during due diligence.

3. Protect Your Intellectual Property

- Ensure trademarks, patents, and copyrights are in place.

- IP protection increases the valuation of your business.

4. Strengthen Your Leadership Team

- A business that runs smoothly without the founder is more appealing to acquirers or IPO investors.

- Train your team to handle key responsibilities.

5. Consult Professionals

- Work with financial advisors, lawyers, and consultants who specialize in exit strategies to avoid costly mistakes.

Dual-Track Approach

Many startups prepare for both an IPO and acquisition simultaneously to maximize exit opportunities.

How It Works:

- The startup prepares for an IPO while remaining open to acquisition offers.

- This approach increases the bargaining power of the founders and investors.

Advantages:

- Flexibility in choosing the best option based on market conditions.

- Forces the company to become IPO-ready, which adds credibility for acquirers.

Challenges:

- Requires additional time, resources, and strategic focus.

Example: Zomato prepared for an IPO while considering strategic partnerships with global investors.

Key Factors to Consider Before Exiting

1. **Timing**: Exit when your business is performing well, and the market conditions are favourable.

2. **Valuation**: Know your company's worth by consulting valuation experts.

3. **Stakeholders**: Ensure your exit benefits not only you but also your employees, investors, and customers.

4. **Post-Exit Plan**: Decide what you'll do after exiting—start a new business, invest, or retire.

Real-Life Lessons from Successful Exits

1. ***BigBasket Acquisition***:
   Tata Digital acquired BigBasket in a $1.2 billion deal in 2021.

BigBasket's focus on operational excellence and customer loyalty made it an attractive acquisition target.

2. ***Oyo's Future IPO Plans***:
Oyo is preparing for its IPO by focusing on profitability, streamlining operations, and improving its valuation metrics.

3. ***Zomato IPO***:
Zomato's IPO in 2021 was a landmark moment for Indian startups, proving that the public market is ready to invest in tech-driven businesses.

Failed Exit Strategy

Snapdeal's merger with Flipkart fell apart due to valuation disagreements and misaligned goals.

Lesson: Align stakeholders and conduct thorough due diligence to avoid missed opportunities.

Conclusion

Planning an exit strategy isn't about leaving your business—it's about ensuring that your hard work continues to deliver value, even after you transition. Whether you choose to sell, merge, or go public, having a well-thought-out exit strategy ensures you make the most of your entrepreneurial journey. Remember, the best exit strategy is one that aligns with your long-term goals and values.

Checklist For Exit Strategies

☐ Have I considered all potential exit strategies (acquisition, IPO, MBO, etc.)?

☐ Is my company financially and operationally ready for due diligence?

☐ Have I protected my intellectual property and ensured compliance?

☐ Do I have clear communication with stakeholders (investors, team, customers) about the exit?

☐ Have I consulted legal and financial professionals to navigate the exit process?

CHAPTER 13

OVERCOMING CHALLENGES

Building a startup is like riding a rollercoaster—there will be exhilarating highs and terrifying lows. Challenges are an inevitable part of the entrepreneurial journey, but how you face them will determine your success. This chapter will focus on identifying common challenges, learning from real-life examples, and providing actionable solutions to navigate these hurdles.

1. Dealing with Failures and Setbacks

The Reality of Failures

Failure is often seen as a dead-end, but in the startup world, it's a stepping stone to success. Many of the world's most successful entrepreneurs faced failures before finding their breakthrough.

Example:

- **Walt Disney**: He was fired from his first job for "lacking imagination." His first animation company also went bankrupt. Today, Disney is one of the biggest media empires globally.

- **Stayzilla**: This Indian homestay platform shut down after facing challenges in scaling and maintaining cash flow. While the company failed, the lessons its founders learned helped them in future ventures.

How to Overcome Failures

1. **Analyze the Root Cause**:

    - Ask tough questions: What went wrong? Was it a market misfit, operational inefficiency, or financial mismanagement?
    - *Example*: Flipkart realized early that weak logistics could hinder its growth. They built Ekart, their in-house delivery system, to solve the issue.

2. **Learn and Adapt**:

    - Treat failure as feedback.
    - *Example*: Kunal Shah, after exiting FreeCharge, reflected on his experiences and founded Cred, learning from his first startup's challenges.

3. **Stay Resilient**:

    - Success often comes to those who refuse to give up.
    - *Quote*: "I have not failed. I've just found 10,000 ways that won't work." – Thomas Edison

4. **Emotional Resilience:**

Emotional resilience is essential for founders facing repeated setbacks.

    - *Mindset Practices*: Focus on mindfulness, journaling, or goal visualization to stay centered.

- ***Real-Life Example***: Jack Ma of Alibaba faced multiple
  failures, including being rejected from dozens of jobs,
  before succeeding.

- ***Encouraging Quote***: *"Success is not final, failure is not
  fatal: It is the courage to continue that counts." – Winston
  Churchill*

2. Managing Finances and Cash Flow

Why Financial Challenges Are Common

One of the most significant reasons startups fail is running out of
money. Poor cash flow management, unexpected expenses, or
delayed revenue can put any business in a tight spot.

Example*:*

- **Zomato**: In its early days, Zomato struggled to generate revenue
  as it offered free listings for restaurants. By introducing
  premium services for restaurants (e.g., advertising and
  subscriptions), they solved their cash flow issues.

How to Handle Financial Challenges

1. **Create a Cash Flow Forecast**:

   - Predict your cash inflows and outflows for the next 6-12
     months.

   - ***Example****:* A SaaS startup like Zoho relies on recurring
     subscriptions, allowing them to predict monthly revenues
     and plan expenses accordingly.

2. **Prioritize Spending**:

   - Focus on essentials like product development and customer acquisition. Avoid unnecessary expenses.

   - ***Example***: Ola cut operational costs by focusing on profitable cities instead of expanding indiscriminately.

3. **Have a Backup Plan**:

   - Build an emergency fund to cover 3-6 months of expenses.

   - Explore alternative funding options, like invoice financing or bridge loans.

4. **Diversify Revenue Streams**:

   - Explore additional ways to generate income, such as introducing premium features or cross-selling.

5. **Negotiate Vendor Terms**:

   - Extend payment terms with suppliers or negotiate discounts for bulk purchases.

6. **Track Key Metrics**:

   - Include examples like gross profit margin or customer acquisition cost (CAC) to help readers identify inefficiencies.

3. Managing Burnout

What is Burnout?

Burnout occurs when prolonged stress leads to physical and emotional exhaustion. Founders often work long hours, juggle multiple roles, and face constant pressure, making them highly susceptible to burnout.

Example:

- **Elon Musk**: Known for his extreme work ethic, Musk once admitted to working 120-hour weeks, which took a toll on his mental health. He later emphasized the importance of balance.

How to Prevent and Manage Burnout

1. ***Delegate Tasks***:

   - Focus on what you do best and delegate the rest.
   - ***Example***: Jeff Bezos stepped back from day-to-day operations at Amazon to focus on long-term strategy.

2. ***Take Breaks***:

   - Schedule downtime to recharge. Even a short vacation can boost productivity.

3. ***Build a Support System***:

   - Surround yourself with mentors, peers, and friends who can provide guidance and encouragement.
   - ***Example***: Falguni Nayar, founder of Nykaa, credits her family's support for helping her navigate challenges.

4. ***Create Work-Life Boundaries***:

   - Use time-blocking techniques to dedicate specific hours to work and personal life.

5. ***Establish No-Work Zones***:

   - Encourage founders and employees to avoid emails or meetings during off-hours.

6. *Build a Delegation Framework*:

- o Train mid-level managers to take ownership of critical functions.

4. Adapting to Change

The Importance of Agility

Markets evolve, customer preferences shift, and unexpected events (like a pandemic) can disrupt your business. Adapting quickly is the key to survival.

Example:

- **Swiggy During COVID-19**: When food delivery demand dropped, Swiggy adapted by launching Instamart, focusing on grocery delivery to cater to lockdown needs. This pivot kept their business afloat.

How to Adapt to Change

1. *Stay Customer-Centric*:

- o Continuously gather feedback to understand evolving customer needs.
- o *Example:* Airbnb shifted its focus to long-term stays and "work-from-anywhere" listings during the pandemic.

2. *Embrace Technology*:

- o Leverage tools and automation to streamline operations and stay competitive.

o *Example*: Lenskart uses AI-powered tools to suggest eyewear based on facial features, improving the customer experience.

3. ***Be Open to Pivoting***:

    o Sometimes, changing your product or business model is necessary.

    o *Example*: Instagram started as a location-based check-in app but pivoted to photo sharing, which led to massive success.

Building Adaptability into Company Culture

Startups that embed adaptability into their culture are more likely to survive industry changes or crises.

- **Encourage Experimentation**: Create an environment where employees feel safe testing new ideas.

- **Foster Cross-Functional Teams**: Enable collaboration between departments to solve problems more creatively.

- **Example**: Google's "*20% Time*" policy encouraged employees to dedicate time to side projects, leading to innovations like Gmail.

Real-Life Case Studies of Overcoming Challenges

1. ***Amazon's Early Losses***:

    o In its initial years, Amazon operated at a loss because it focused on scaling. Jeff Bezos famously reinvested profits

into expanding the business. This long-term strategy paid
off as Amazon became one of the world's largest
companies.

2. *Netflix's Pivot*:

- Netflix started as a DVD rental service but saw the shift toward digital streaming early. By adapting their model, they became a global leader in streaming, leaving competitors like Blockbuster behind.

3. *Paytm's Survival During Demonetization*:

- While demonetization in India disrupted many businesses, Paytm thrived by offering digital payment solutions when cash was scarce. This adaptability helped them gain millions of new users.

4. *Zerodha's Minimalist Approach*:

- Zerodha thrived during volatile market periods by keeping operational costs low and focusing on long-term customer education.

5. *Tesla's Early Struggles*:

- Despite production delays and near bankruptcy, Tesla succeeded by doubling down on innovation and customer loyalty.

5. Turning Challenges into Opportunities

Why Challenges Are Growth Opportunities

Every challenge forces you to think creatively, innovate, and push
boundaries. Instead of seeing problems as obstacles, treat them as
opportunities to learn and grow.

Example:

- **Apple's Near Bankruptcy**: In 1997, Apple was on the brink of bankruptcy. Steve Jobs returned to the company, streamlined operations, and focused on innovation, launching iconic products like the iMac, iPod, and iPhone. Today, Apple is one of the most valuable companies in the world.

Checklist: Overcoming Challenges in Your Startup

☐ Have I created a detailed cash flow forecast and backup financial plan?

☐ Am I addressing burnout through delegation, breaks, and long-term solutions?

☐ Have I built a culture of adaptability in my team?

☐ Am I actively learning from setbacks and using them to refine my strategy?

☐ Do I have a support network of mentors, peers, or advisors to guide me?

Conclusion

Challenges are inevitable, but they are also the stepping stones to growth and success. By learning to manage failures, finances, burnout, and change, you'll not only survive but thrive in your entrepreneurial journey. Remember, it's not the absence of challenges that defines successful entrepreneurs—it's their ability to overcome them with resilience, creativity, and determination.

CHAPTER 14

REAL-LIFE STARTUP LESSONS

The journey of building a startup is full of highs and lows, triumphs and setbacks. While every business is unique, there are valuable lessons to be learned from the successes and failures of others. This chapter dives deep into real-life case studies, highlighting what startups did right, the mistakes they made, and how you can apply these insights to your entrepreneurial journey.

1. Case Studies of Successful Startups

Case Study 1: Flipkart – Building an E-Commerce Empire

The Journey:
Flipkart started in 2007 as an online bookstore, founded by Sachin and Binny Bansal. They later diversified into electronics, fashion, and home goods, becoming India's leading e-commerce platform.

Key Lessons:

1. **Focus on Customer Experience**:

- o Flipkart introduced cash-on-delivery in India, addressing the lack of trust in online payments.

  - o They prioritized fast delivery and hassle-free returns, which earned customer loyalty.

2. **Invest in Infrastructure**:

  - o They built **Ekart**, their in-house logistics arm, to solve delivery challenges in a fragmented market.

  - o This allowed them to offer faster, more reliable service compared to competitors.

3. **Know When to Partner or Exit**:

  - o Flipkart sold a 77% stake to Walmart in 2018 for $16 billion, a strategic move that provided resources for future growth while rewarding early investors.

What You Can Learn:

- Understand your customer's pain points and address them innovatively.

- Build infrastructure early to support scaling.

- Be open to partnerships or acquisitions when it benefits your startup.

Case Study 2: Zomato – Innovating in the Food Tech Space

The Journey:

Zomato began in 2008 as an online platform to browse restaurant menus. Over time, they expanded into food delivery, online table booking, and hyperlocal delivery services.

Key Lessons:

1. **Adapt to Market Needs**:

   - Zomato pivoted from being a menu aggregator to a full-fledged food delivery platform, responding to customer demand.

2. **Leverage Branding**:

   - Their quirky social media posts and relatable humour helped them build a strong, memorable brand.

3. **Expand Internationally with Focus**:

   - Instead of expanding everywhere at once, Zomato strategically entered markets like the UAE and Australia, where they saw high potential for growth.

What You Can Learn:

- Be flexible and willing to pivot based on market trends.

- Invest in building a relatable brand that connects with your audience.

- Scale thoughtfully, focusing on markets with high ROI.

Case Study 3: Nykaa – Disrupting the Beauty Industry

The Journey:

Founded by Falguni Nayar in 2012, Nykaa started as an online beauty retailer. Today, it's a multi-channel beauty platform with its own private-label brands, physical stores, and an IPO valuation of over $13 billion.

Key Lessons:

1. **Identify and Own a Niche**:

- ○ Nykaa focused on the underserved beauty and wellness segment in India, catering to both luxury and affordable categories.

2. **Omni-Channel Presence**:

   - ○ They combined e-commerce with physical stores to create a seamless shopping experience for customers.

3. **Leverage Content for Customer Engagement**:

   - ○ Nykaa's YouTube tutorials, beauty blogs, and influencer collaborations built trust and attracted a loyal audience.

What You Can Learn:

- Choose a niche market and dominate it.

- Use content to educate and engage customers.

- Diversify your revenue streams with multiple sales channels.

2. Common Mistakes to Avoid

1. Ignoring Market Research

Many startups fail because they build a product they *think* customers want, instead of validating it through research.

Example:
Stayzilla, a homestay platform, misjudged the demand for budget homestays in smaller Indian cities. Despite early success, they couldn't scale due to low demand and financial mismanagement.

Lesson:
Conduct thorough market research and validate your idea with real customers before scaling.

2. Scaling Too Quickly

Expanding too fast without a solid foundation can backfire.

Example:
Grofers (now Blinkit) initially struggled when they expanded to multiple cities too quickly without understanding local logistics and customer preferences. They had to pull back and refocus on core markets before scaling again.

Lesson:
Focus on building strong operations in your initial markets before scaling.

3. Underestimating Cash Flow

Many startups burn through cash without planning for sustainability.

Example:
Housing.com raised significant funding but spent heavily on marketing and operational costs, leading to financial instability.

Lesson:
Monitor your burn rate and prioritize profitability over flashy marketing campaigns.

4. Ignoring Unit Economics

Example:

Uber faced challenges in certain markets because subsidies for riders and drivers weren't sustainable.

Lesson:

Understand the cost per unit and ensure profitability at scale.

5. Overemphasis on Funding

Example:

Many startups, like Housing.com, burned through large funding rounds without achieving profitability, leading to financial instability.

Lesson:

Focus on creating sustainable revenue streams before scaling aggressively.

3. Key Takeaways from Global Startups

1. Airbnb – The Power of Storytelling

Airbnb's early growth came from creating a strong emotional connection with users. They told stories of hosts and travellers, showing how their platform created unique experiences.

Lesson:
Use storytelling to build a connection with your audience and differentiate your brand.

2. Tesla – Vision Drives Growth

Tesla's success isn't just about electric cars—it's about Elon Musk's bold vision for a sustainable future.

Lesson:
A compelling vision can inspire customers, employees, and investors alike.

3. Slack – Solving a Real Problem

Slack focused on solving communication issues for teams. By building a simple, intuitive product and offering free trials, they gained rapid adoption.

Lesson:
Focus on solving a specific, tangible problem. Let your product's value drive adoption.

4. *Building Your Own Lessons*

Every entrepreneur's journey is unique, and the most valuable lessons often come from personal experience. Here's how you can build your own repository of insights:

1. **Reflect Regularly**:
   - After every major milestone or setback, reflect on what worked and what didn't.
   - *Example*: At the end of a marketing campaign, analyze metrics like ROI and customer acquisition costs to identify strengths and weaknesses.

2. **Learn from Others**:
   - Read books, attend webinars, or listen to podcasts by successful entrepreneurs.
   - *Example*: Books like *The Lean Startup* by Eric Ries offer practical frameworks for building and scaling startups.

3. **Stay Adaptable**:
   - No lesson is universal—adapt strategies to fit your unique circumstances.

Checklist: Real-Life Startup Lessons

1. **Customer-Centric Approach**: Always prioritize solving real customer problems.

2. **Focus on Financial Discipline**: Monitor your cash flow and spend wisely.

3. **Be Ready to Pivot**: Don't be afraid to change your strategy if the market demands it.

4. **Build a Scalable Model**: Test operations in one market before expanding.

5. **Learn from Failures**: Every setback is an opportunity to improve.

Conclusion

The stories of successful startups teach us that there's no one-size-fits-all formula for success. It takes persistence, adaptability, and the willingness to learn from both wins and failures. As you navigate your entrepreneurial journey, remember that every challenge is an opportunity to grow, and every success is a reminder of why you started.

RESOURCES AND TOOLS

Starting and scaling a business requires the right resources, tools, and frameworks. This section provides practical, actionable tools to help you streamline processes, save time, and make informed decisions at every stage of your entrepreneurial journey. From business templates to marketing tools, these resources are designed to support you in achieving your startup goals.

1. Business Templates

Having ready-to-use templates can save you time and ensure you don't miss critical details when starting your business. Here are some essential templates you can use:

Business Plan Template

A comprehensive template that covers:

- Executive summary

- Market analysis

- Financial projections

- Marketing and sales strategy

Recommended Tool: Use platforms like Canva or templates from HubSpot to create visually appealing business plans.

Pitch Deck Template

A pitch deck is crucial for presenting your idea to investors. It should include:

- Problem and solution
- Business model
- Market size and opportunity
- Team and traction

Recommended Tool: Slidebean and Visme offer easy-to-edit pitch deck templates with professional designs.

Financial Planning Spreadsheet

Track your income, expenses, and cash flow with this simple spreadsheet. Key features include:

- Monthly revenue and expense tracking
- Break-even analysis
- Forecasting tools

Recommended Tool: Use Google Sheets or Microsoft Excel templates for financial planning.

2. Marketing Tools

Marketing is a critical component of growth. These tools can help you reach and engage your audience effectively:

Social Media Management

- **Tool**: Buffer, Hootsuite, or Zoho Social

- **Why**: Schedule posts, track engagement, and analyze performance across platforms like Instagram, LinkedIn, and Twitter.

Email Marketing

- **Tool**: Mailchimp or ConvertKit
- **Why**: Create automated email campaigns to nurture leads and keep your audience engaged.

SEO Tools

- **Tool**: SEMrush, Ahrefs, or Google Keyword Planner
- **Why**: Optimize your website for search engines and drive organic traffic.

Graphic Design

- **Tool**: Canva or Adobe Express
- **Why**: Create professional graphics for your website, social media, and ads, even without design skills.

3. Productivity and Collaboration Tools

As your team grows, staying organized and ensuring clear communication is vital.

Project Management

- **Tool**: Trello, Asana, or ClickUp
- **Why**: Manage tasks, track progress, and collaborate with your team seamlessly.

Communication

- **Tool**: Slack or Microsoft Teams

- **Why**: Keep your team connected and improve real-time communication.

Time Management

- **Tool**: Toggl or Clockify

- **Why**: Track time spent on tasks and improve productivity.

4. Financial Tools

Efficient financial management can make or break your startup. Use these tools to stay on top of your finances:

Accounting and Invoicing

- **Tool**: QuickBooks, Tally, or Zoho Books

- **Why**: Simplify invoicing, expense tracking, and tax filing.

Payment Processing

- **Tool**: Razorpay, Stripe, or PayPal

- **Why**: Offer secure payment options to your customers, whether online or offline.

Budgeting and Expense Tracking

- **Tool**: Expenslfy or YNAB (You Need A Budget)

- **Why**: Monitor expenses and manage budgets effectively.

5. Learning Resources

Continuous learning is essential for staying ahead. Here are some platforms and books to help you grow:

Online Learning Platforms

- **Coursera and Udemy**: Learn about marketing, finance, and leadership.
- **Y Combinator Startup School**: Access free courses and resources for startups.
- **LinkedIn Learning**: Explore courses on sales, branding, and business strategy.

Books

- *The Lean Startup* by Eric Ries: A guide to building businesses through innovation and iteration.
- *Zero to One* by Peter Thiel: Insights on creating unique, world-changing businesses.
- *Shoe Dog* by Phil Knight: The memoir of Nike's founder, full of lessons on resilience and creativity.

6. Networking and Mentorship

Building connections and finding mentors can open doors to opportunities and insights:

Startup Communities

- **TiE (The Indus Entrepreneurs)**: A global network for entrepreneurs.
- **Startup India Hub**: Resources and networking opportunities for Indian startups.
- **AngelList**: A platform to connect with investors and mentors.

Events and Competitions

- Attend events like TechCrunch Disrupt, Web Summit, or local startup meetups to connect with industry leaders and investors.

Mentorship Platforms

- **MentorKart**: Find industry mentors to guide you through challenges.

- **Clarity.fm**: Book calls with experts across various industries.

7. Funding Platforms

Raising funds is a critical milestone. These platforms can help you find investors:

Crowdfunding

- **Kickstarter**: Raise funds for innovative products.

- **Ketto**: Ideal for social impact startups in India.

Angel and Venture Capital

- **AngelList**: Connect with angel investors and VCs.

- **LetsVenture**: Simplify fundraising for startups in India.

Grants and Government Support

- Explore schemes like **Startup India** and **MSME** subsidies for funding and tax benefits.

8. Tools for Scaling

When you're ready to scale, these tools can help you streamline and expand operations:

E-Commerce Platforms

- **Shopify or WooCommerce**: Build your online store easily.

Customer Relationship Management (CRM)

- **HubSpot or Zoho CRM**: Manage leads, sales pipelines, and customer relationships.

Analytics Tools

- **Google Analytics**: Track website performance and user behavior.

- **Mixpanel**: Analyze customer interactions with your product.

9. Templates, Checklists, and Useful Links

Startup Checklist

- Idea validation: ☑

- Business registration: ☑

- MVP development: ☑

- Marketing strategy: ☑

Useful Links

- Startup India Portal: Government resources for Indian startups.

- SEMRush Blog: Tips on digital marketing and SEO.

- YC Startup Library: Free guides and videos from Y Combinator.

Conclusion

The right tools and resources can be the difference between chaos and clarity in your startup journey. By leveraging these resources, you can save time, reduce costs, and make smarter decisions. Remember, tools are only as effective as how you use them—stay focused, stay curious, and keep building toward success.

Let me know if you'd like more specific templates, links, or resources added to this section!

CONCLUSION: YOUR ROADMAP TO SUCCESS

The journey of building a startup is much more than just running a business—it's about solving real problems, making an impact, and growing into the person you're meant to be. By now, you've explored the foundational steps to turn your idea into reality, learned from real-life examples, and seen the challenges and triumphs of entrepreneurship. This roadmap isn't just theoretical—it's actionable, proven, and designed to help you succeed.

Your Roadmap to Success

Here's a quick summary of the journey you've been guided through in this book:

1. Starting with an Idea

- Identify real problems and validate your idea to ensure it meets market needs.

- Remember, every great business started with a simple idea.

    - ***Example****:* Ola started because the founders struggled to find a reliable taxi in Bangalore.

2. Laying the Foundation

- Define your vision, mission, and values to guide your startup.

- Choose the right legal structure and register your business properly.

- *Example:* Nykaa's focus on empowering women shaped its identity and culture, which still resonates with its audience today.

3. Growing Step by Step

- Build your product with feedback from real customers.

- Market your business smartly, focusing on your audience's needs and preferences.

  - *Example*: Zomato's journey from menu listings to food delivery showed the power of listening to market demand.

4. Preparing for Challenges and Scaling

- Manage your finances wisely and prepare for uncertainties.

- Scale responsibly by testing new markets and automating operations.

  - *Example:* Flipkart scaled responsibly by building its in-house logistics arm, Ekart, ensuring they could handle rapid growth.

5. Long-Term Planning

- Plan your exit strategy to maximize returns and ensure your business thrives even after you move on.

- Learn to adapt to market shifts and new challenges.

  - *Example*: Airbnb pivoted during the pandemic to cater to long-term stays, proving their agility.

Final Words of Encouragement

As you embark on your entrepreneurial journey, remember that every success story starts with one bold decision: to begin. Here's how to maintain the momentum and keep moving forward:

1. Believe in Yourself

Your belief in your vision is the foundation of everything. There will be naysayers, obstacles, and self-doubt, but your conviction will keep you going.

- *Example*: Colonel Sanders faced over 1,000 rejections before someone believed in his fried chicken recipe. Today, KFC is a global brand.

2. Embrace the Process

The path to success is rarely a straight line. Celebrate small wins, learn from failures, and treat each step as a learning experience.

- *Example*: Tesla faced delays and financial challenges in launching the Model 3, but Elon Musk's relentless focus turned it into one of the best-selling electric cars globally.

3. Stay Resilient During Challenges

Every successful entrepreneur has faced failures, but their resilience helped them persevere.

- *Example*: Byju Raveendran, the founder of Byju's, started by teaching a small group of students. His journey wasn't easy, but his persistence turned Byju's into a global edtech giant.

4. Focus on Impact

The businesses that leave a legacy are those that prioritize making a difference. Your startup has the power to solve problems and improve lives.

- *Example*: Paytm revolutionized digital payments in India, particularly during demonetization, making a tangible impact on how people transact.

5. Take Action Now

The biggest difference between a dreamer and a doer is action. You've already done the groundwork by reading this book—now it's time to take the first step.

- Whether it's writing your business plan, building your MVP, or pitching to investors, start small and stay consistent.

Your Journey, Your Story

You're now equipped with the tools, strategies, and insights to navigate your entrepreneurial journey. The world needs more problem-solvers like you—people who are willing to take risks, innovate, and make a difference.

As you move forward, remember that success isn't just about achieving goals—it's about the growth, learning, and impact you create along the way. One day, your story will inspire others just like the examples you've read in this book.

Here's to your success, your growth, and the incredible journey ahead.

A Personal Note from the Author

"When I left my job in the Merchant Navy in 2019, I was unsure about the future. But what kept me going was my desire for freedom and my passion for building something meaningful. The journey wasn't easy—I faced doubts, challenges, and setbacks—but each step taught me something valuable. Today, I've had the privilege of helping businesses grow and sharing what I've learned with aspiring entrepreneurs like you. If there's one thing I've realized, it's this: success belongs to those who dare to start. And now, it's your turn to start your journey."

Wishing You All the Success in the World!

Take that first step today. The world is waiting for your idea to make an impact.

Good luck!

ACKNOWLEDGMENTS

No entrepreneurial journey is ever a solo effort. Behind every success, there is an entire ecosystem of people who inspire, guide, and support us along the way. This book, and my journey as an entrepreneur, wouldn't have been possible without the contributions, love, and encouragement of so many remarkable individuals.

A Note of Gratitude to You

First and foremost, I want to thank **you, the reader**, for picking up this book and trusting me to be a part of your entrepreneurial journey. Your belief in your dreams, your hunger for knowledge, and your willingness to take bold steps inspire me. You are the reason this book exists. If my experiences, stories, and insights have helped you in any way, then my purpose for writing this book has been fulfilled.

To My Family

To my family, who stood by me when I made the life-changing decision to leave my secure career in the Merchant Navy to pursue entrepreneurship—thank you for believing in me, even when the path wasn't clear. You've been my strongest pillars, celebrating my wins and holding me up during the hardest days.

When I doubted myself, you reminded me why I started this journey. Without your unwavering support, this dream might have remained just that—a dream.

To My Friends and Supporters

To the friends who never stopped cheering for me—you've been my second family. Your constant encouragement, honest feedback, and the occasional reality checks have played an enormous role in shaping my growth as an entrepreneur and writer.

The late-night brainstorming sessions, your willingness to listen to my crazy ideas, and your belief in my potential kept me going. Thank you for being my sounding boards, critics, and motivators.

To My Mentors and Role Models

To the mentors who shared their wisdom, both in the Merchant Navy and in my entrepreneurial journey—thank you for being my compass. Your guidance taught me how to navigate uncertainty with confidence, how to turn setbacks into opportunities, and how to stay grounded in the face of success.

Key Lesson: Having someone who has walked the path before you is invaluable. If you're reading this, find a mentor who inspires you—they can change your life.

To My Merchant Navy Days

A special thank you to my years in the Merchant Navy, which taught me the value of discipline, resilience, and leadership. Working as an Officer wasn't just a career—it was a training ground for life. The long nights at sea, the tough decisions, and the teamwork prepared me for the highs and lows of entrepreneurship.

Leaving that career in 2019 was one of the hardest decisions of my life. But it was also one of the best. The lessons I learned during that time are woven into the fabric of my entrepreneurial journey and this book.

To Fellow Entrepreneurs and Innovators

To every founder, dreamer, and creator I've met or worked with along the way—thank you for sharing your stories, your struggles, and your triumphs. You've reminded me that entrepreneurship is not just about building businesses; it's about building communities and solving real problems.

Your passion and grit have been a constant source of inspiration for me, and I'm honored to share this journey with you.

To the Team Behind This Book

A heartfelt thank you to everyone who helped bring this book to life:

- To the **editors and reviewers** who refined my thoughts into clear, actionable advice.
- To the **designers** who turned my words into a visually appealing experience.
- To the **beta readers** who provided feedback and helped me see the book from fresh perspectives.

This book is as much yours as it is mine.

A Message to You, the Dreamer

As I sit here reflecting on my journey, I realize how similar it might be to yours. When I left my job in the Merchant Navy, I had no guarantees, no roadmap, and no safety net. What I did have was a burning desire for freedom and the determination to build something of my own.

It wasn't easy—there were days of doubt, fear, and failure. But every challenge taught me something valuable, and every small win brought me closer to my dreams. Today, as I write this, I can tell you with confidence: the risks were worth it.

If you're reading this and wondering whether you should take the leap, let me tell you—**you can do it**. You have everything you need within you to build something extraordinary. Trust yourself, start small, and keep going, even when the path seems unclear.

Remember: Success isn't about having all the answers; it's about taking action despite the uncertainties.

Final Words

This book is not just a guide; it's a piece of my journey, and I hope it becomes a part of yours too. I hope it serves as a reminder that no dream is too big and no challenge is too great if you have the courage to keep moving forward.

To everyone who has been a part of this journey—thank you. And to you, the entrepreneur reading this: your story is just beginning, and I can't wait to see the incredible impact you're going to create.

With gratitude and belief in your success,
Your Author

9 798889 724099